THIS IS YOUR BRAIN ON STEREOTYPES

HOW SCIENCE IS TACKLING UNCONSCIOUS BIAS

TANYA LLOYD KYI
DREW SHANNON

Kids Can Press

To my husband, Min Kyi — T.L.K.

ACKNOWLEDGMENTS

Creating a book about stereotypes requires an entire team of editors, experts and sensitivity readers. This project would never have been accomplished without the insightful contributions of Jennifer Stokes, Kathleen Keenan, Genie MacLeod, Dr. Frances Aboud, Wilfred Burton, Jessica Pryde, Margaret Kingsbury, Shana Hayes and DoEun Kwon. Thank you also to Marie Bartholomew and Barb Kelly for helping bring the book to life.

Kids Can Press gratefully acknowledges the financial support of the Government of Ontario, through Ontario Creates; the Ontario Arts Council; the Canada Council for the Arts; and the Government of Canada for our publishing activity.

Published in Canada and the U.S. by Kids Can Press Ltd.
25 Dockside Drive, Toronto, ON M5A 0B5

Kids Can Press is a Corus Entertainment Inc. company

www.kidscanpress.com

The artwork in this book was rendered digitally.
The text is set in Picadilly.

Edited by Jennifer Stokes and Kathleen Keenan
Designed by Barb Kelly and Marie Bartholomew

Printed and bound in Shenzhen, China, in 3/2020
by C & C Offset

CM 20 0 9 8 7 6 5 4 3 2 1

Library and Archives Canada Cataloguing in Publication

Title: This is your brain on stereotypes : how science is tackling unconscious bias / Tanya Lloyd Kyi, Drew Shannon.

Names: Kyi, Tanya Lloyd, 1973– author. | Shannon, Drew, 1988– illustrator.

Description: Includes bibliographical references and index.

Identifiers: Canadiana 20190206896 | ISBN 9781525300165 (hardcover)

Subjects: LCSH: Stereotypes (Social psychology) — Juvenile literature. | LCSH: Discrimination — Juvenile literature.

Classification: LCC BF323.S63 K95 2020 | DDC j303.3/85 — dc23

Contents

Introduction 4

Chapter 1: Perception Deception 6

Chapter 2: Secret Messages 20

Chapter 3: Me, Myself and I 37

Chapter 4: Change-Makers 49

Chapter 5: Rewiring the Mind 61

Conclusion: The Chances for Change 77

Further Reading 80

Selected Sources 81

Index 86

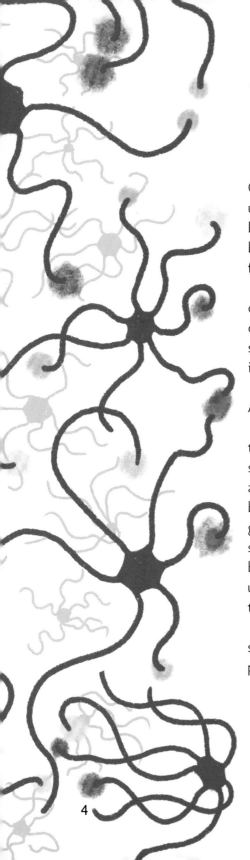

Introduction

Our brains constantly sort and label the world around us. It begins when we're babies. Those four-legged barking things? They're dogs. The bouncy things are balls. Toys are different from food, and food is different from milk.

We need these categories. Without them, we'd open our closets each morning and wonder which items of clothing go on our legs and which go on our arms. We'd stare into our desk drawers trying to figure out which items write and which ones erase.

But our brains don't only sort *things*. They sort *people*. And that's where life gets complicated.

When we group people into a category, and assume they all share certain traits, that's called a stereotype. Some stereotypes seem to be based on facts. For example, imagine a group of kids playing video games. Are you picturing boys? If so, you're not wrong. About 60 percent of regular gamers are male. But not *all* gamers are male, and not *all* stereotypes are true. By relying on people-categories in our brains, we can make false assumptions. We can even act unfairly toward certain people, all because we've jumped to bad conclusions.

When a large majority of people, or even a whole society, holds the same unfair stereotypes, real people pay the price.

- In the United States, young black men are nine times more likely than white men to be killed by police.
- Girls do just as well as boys in high school science. But in countries ranging from Belgium to Sweden and Australia to Germany, far fewer girls graduate with post-secondary science degrees.
- In Canada, kids living on First Nations reserves receive less government money for education and health care than other Canadian kids.
- American LGBTQ+ youth are twice as likely as their peers to be bullied at school.

None of this is fair. And much of it results from the ways we categorize minority groups. So here's an idea: Let's stop sorting people based on their race, gender or sexual orientation. Let's end stereotypes. Let's change laws, school rules and our own brains. Quick!

Unfortunately, it's not that easy. Stereotypes are hard to recognize — and even harder to erase. People simply don't know how to fix these problems.

That's where science comes in.

For more than a hundred years, scientists have been trying to figure out how we classify people, and why. Recently, they've kicked their research into high gear. They're exploring the ways neural pathways inside our brains affect how we create and react to stereotypes. They're delving into the reasons we continue to sort and judge others, even when we're trying to improve. And, slowly but surely, they're finding ways we can rewire our minds — and our societies.

It's going to be a long process. But hopefully, these scientists (plus activists, doctors, teachers, politicians and even readers like you) can help make the world more fair for everyone.

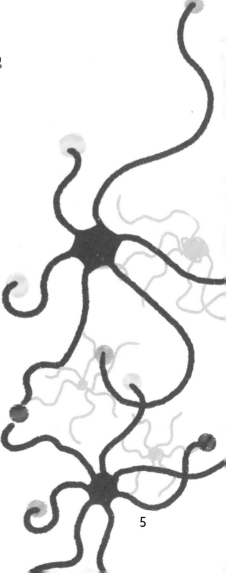

Chapter 1

Perception Deception

Some scientists believe stereotypes are part of our genetic code and evolved to help us recognize members of our own families or tribes. This would have been a vital skill thousands of years ago.

Other researchers argue that we're not born understanding stereotypes — we learn them from our parents and absorb them from society. Because we find them useful, we learn them quickly and we're reluctant to give them up.

Either way, we've all got them.

Think about these labels:

 • terrorist
 • senior citizen
 • hip-hop artist
 • environmentalist

Each of these probably conjures an image in your mind. If you could capture those images and compare them with pictures from the minds of your friends, you'd find many similarities. Seniors use glasses; terrorists carry guns. Hip-hop artists have tattoos; environmentalists eat tofu.

These snapshots serve as mental shortcuts, and they're sometimes useful. If you invite your new environmentalist friend over for lunch, the stereotype in your brain might help you remember to ask, "Hey, are you a vegetarian?"

In other ways, stereotypes are scary. They can lead us to judge people unfairly, before we really know them.

Cranium Crackpots

In the 1800s, scientists were super committed to figuring out how people fit into categories. Some measured people's craniums, trying to prove that skull shape and brain size affected intelligence. Others measured nose width or the space between people's eyes.

There was just one teensy problem: those scientists were trying to show that upper-class white people were best. They were all trying to justify their own stereotypes!

A few scientists took this sort of research even further. One of the most influential was an English guy named Francis Galton. He studied everything you can think of: statistics, society, the brain, geography, weather patterns and human hearing. He figured out how to classify fingerprints and how to track storms.

Francis's cousin was Charles Darwin. Yup, THE Charles Darwin, the guy who came up with the theory of evolution. Thanks to his famous cuz, Francis knew that traits are passed from parents to offspring. He knew that the strongest creatures are best able to survive.

These concepts prompted one of Francis's wackier ideas: eugenics. He believed that if smart, successful people passed on their traits to their children, then it would be easy to improve civilization. The government should just pay smart people to have more kids! If the most brilliant parents hatched lots of brilliant kids, the world's population would become more intelligent. (This was not so good for less bright people, who would be discouraged from starting families. But Francis didn't seem worried about them.)

Outside the Box

There are four words that researchers use to talk about the ways we categorize and misjudge people.

Bias

Way back in the 1530s, *bias* just meant a slanted line. Today, we also use it to talk about off-kilter judgments. When you make a biased decision, it's because your own beliefs have slanted your thinking. If you hate all green vegetables, for example, you're probably biased *against* broccoli and *toward* carrots.

Discrimination

By choosing those carrots for dinner instead of broccoli, you're discriminating *between* vegetables. That use of the word dates back hundreds of years. But in the 1800s, as activists fought to end slavery in the United States, the term gained another use: discriminating *against*. Or treating a person or a group of people unfairly because of their race. Today, we recognize many other reasons for discrimination, including gender and sexual orientation.

Prejudice

This means pre-judging something without trying it first. If you've never tasted eggplant, but you hate it, you hold a prejudice. Or maybe you had one burnt eggplant, and now you assume all eggplant

dishes are terrible. Again, that's a pre-judgment, or prejudice. This isn't a big deal if you're talking about vegetables. It *is* a big deal if you're talking about an entire race, religion or class of people.

Stereotype

Until the 1920s, a stereotype was an exact copy made by a printing press. Then along came Walter Lippmann, an American newspaper writer and a philosopher. Walter believed that readers created pictures in their minds based on their own experiences. He suggested that when people read newspaper articles or listened to politicians, they didn't judge the information clearly. Instead, they made it fit their own mental images. They made a copy, or a stereotype, based on the way they understood the world. For example, if broccoli was the only green vegetable they'd ever tried, they might assume spinach, cabbage and sprouts all taste like broccoli.

When Walter Lippmann created this new definition of stereotype, he wasn't talking about race. But it didn't take long for his word to catch on. After all, people were struggling against this sort of categorization in countries around the world. In the United States, women gained the right to vote in 1920, but — through a tricky list of taxes and tests — the Southern states managed to keep black women from casting ballots. Around the same time, Mahatma Gandhi was protesting British rule in India and trying to end centuries of discrimination there. Canada was busy banning Chinese immigration and severely limiting Japanese immigration. And something even worse was brewing in Europe ...

Eugenics Gets Ugly

From the 1890s to the mid-1900s, people all over the world toyed with the idea of creating stronger humans, controlling which people had kids and encouraging a master race. This was before there were even words to talk about stereotypes. But some scientists, professors and politicians were hard at work creating them.

Wilhelm Schallmayer, Germany, 1891

He thought that by treating sick and "weak" people, doctors were leading to the downfall of civilization. It would be better to help the strong and let the others wither away.

Georges Vacher de Lapouge, France, 1899

This guy believed tall, strong, white people were best, and dark-skinned Mediterranean types weren't so smart. He suggested keeping them separate so the world would have high-class leaders and lower-class workers. He spoke six languages, so he could explain this in English, German ...

Charles and Gertrude Davenport, United States, 1910

These super-rich Americans said upper-class white people should have many children. Lower-class people — especially immigrants — should have none. They even suggested operating on "unfit" mothers to make sure they couldn't have kids.

Alfred Ploetz, Germany, 1933

Alfred thought the government should decide which parents were strong and healthy enough to have kids. And he believed Adolf Hitler was exactly the leader to put his ideas into action.

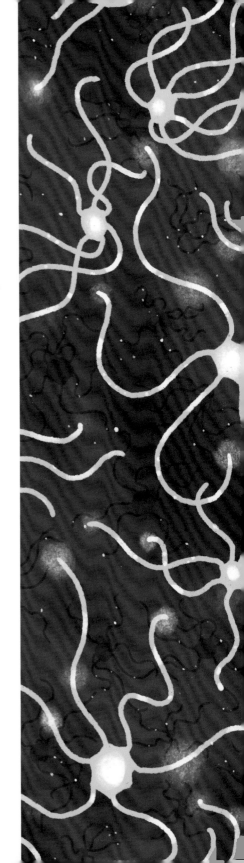

There were more than nine million Jewish people in Europe in 1933, when Hitler took power. By the time World War II ended in 1945, the Nazis had murdered more than six million.

Adolf Hitler and his Nazi party took power in Germany in 1933. Influenced by many researchers and writers of the time, Hitler decided to create a master race. The world would be led by tall, strong, blue-eyed "Aryans." At the very bottom of the race hierarchy would be Jewish people.

The Nazis began by excluding Jewish people from society — banning them from owning land, for example. They then isolated them in a system of more than 40 000 ghettos, detention sites and prisons. Finally, they started systematically killing Jewish people in extermination camps and gas chambers.

Jewish people weren't the only group targeted by Hitler's Nazis. About 200 000 Roma people (then known as "gypsies") were killed, along with communists, homosexuals, Jehovah's Witnesses and hundreds of thousands of those with mental and physical disabilities.

Hitler tried to create a world based on stereotyping, prejudice and discrimination in their most extreme forms.

Glass Houses

In the 1930s, researchers at Princeton University in the United States asked students to match ten ethnic groups with traits that described them. Here are some of the results:

- 79 percent of students thought Jewish people were shrewd
- 78 percent thought Germans were scientific-minded
- 75 percent thought black people were lazy
- 54 percent thought Turks were cruel

Obviously, Germans weren't the only ones holding biased views based on race and ethnicity. Stereotypes were flourishing on both sides of the Atlantic.

Emergency Re-Think

Screeech! Hold the presses! Something had gone seriously wrong. Ideas about eugenics and master races hadn't led to a better world. Instead, millions had been slaughtered.

World War II made people around the world realize that stereotypes could be dangerous. Politicians and newspaper editors, business magnates and religious leaders all started to wonder: What had happened inside those Nazi brains? What prompted such efforts to exterminate another race? And what about the people who quietly watched it all unfold — what was going on in *their* minds?

Theodor Adorno had personal reasons for asking these questions. Before the war, he was a respected professor at the University of Frankfurt in Germany. He taught philosophy, wrote about culture and composed classical music. Life was pretty good ... until the Nazis took control.

Theodor was Jewish.

In 1934, he fled to England, then to the United States. He took a position as co-director of the Research Project on Social Discrimination at the University of California, Berkeley. For seven years, from 1941 to 1948, he tried to figure out what the heck had happened. How had the world watched while Jewish people were excluded from society, persecuted and eventually murdered?

In 1950, Theodor co-wrote a book called *The Authoritarian Personality*. He argued that authoritarians — forceful, know-it-all leaders like Hitler — saw the world in strict categories. ("Me leader. You follower.") They valued obedience and structure. It was easy for these types of people to stereotype.

Theodor based many of his ideas on his own experiences and observations. But over the past few decades, scientists have conducted studies and collected data to test his theories. They've proven his conclusions correct, again and again.

- Studies in many countries have shown that, yes, right-wing authoritarianism leads to prejudice.
- People who strongly believe they belong to a better, more powerful group are more likely to discriminate against weaker groups.
- People who think in absolutes — black and white, right and wrong, high-class and low-class — are more likely to discriminate.

An American professor named Gordon Allport gave racism research another big boost in 1954 with a book called *The Nature of Prejudice*. He realized that a stereotype isn't a single fact or sentence in a person's brain. He said it is more like a habitual way of thinking about the world, or something you mindlessly absorbed from those around you.

Sketchy Thinking

Draw a picture of a math professor. Do it quickly, without thinking, and don't read any further until you're finished. Got it?

Now, check your picture for these stereotypical traits: Does your math professor wear glasses? Is he male? White? Skinny? Nerdy? Does he have white hair that sticks straight into the air? These are all common stereotypes. They're no big deal if you're sketching. But they *are* a big deal if you're a girl considering which career to choose. Would a twelve-year-old girl see her future in the picture you've drawn?

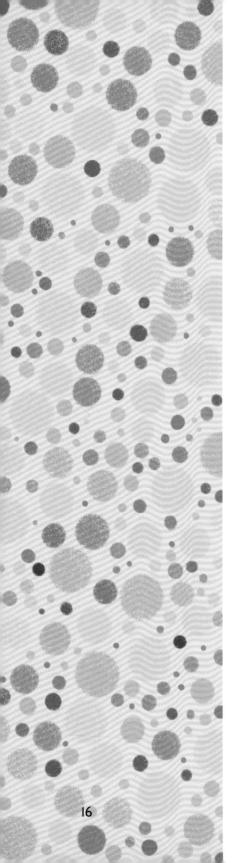

Ins and Outs

Congratulations! Your soccer team made the city finals! And what a group. Your striker is quick and coordinated. Your goalkeeper is tough but fair. You're proud to be part of this team.

The tournament begins. You win your first game, no problem. The opposition is slow and uncoordinated. But ouch! You lose your second match. Not because of any lack of skill. Those other players are downright mean. They throw elbows at every opportunity. The ref is blind not to see their fouls.

Does any of this sound familiar? It's an exaggerated description of something scientists call the out-group homogeneity effect. That's a fancy way of saying that people usually find their own team members to be uniquely talented, while outsiders get lumped together as losers.

It's not just about soccer. In-group and out-group thinking applies whether you're in a dance troupe or on a basketball team, in chess club or on student council. We humans assume our own groups are best.

Princeton University researchers first studied this in the 1970s and '80s. They found that members of a group recognize the differences within that group. (On your soccer team, you might say, "Joanna's quick. She's our best striker." Or "Karim's ability to see the whole field makes him the perfect midfielder.") But group members lump outsiders into broad categories. (In soccer terms, "Those opposing players suck.")

Why do we jump to conclusions like this? Mostly because it makes us feel good. Being a member of the in-group is a big self-esteem boost.

Color~~blind~~

News flash: *People like belonging! They think their own groups are best!*

If you read those headlines, you might say, "Duh. So obvious. Did scientists really spend decades researching that?"

Yes, they did. And they gave it a fancy name: intergroup bias.

But here's the surprising part. It takes only tiny details to make you feel biased toward your own crowd. For example, if half the kids in your class are given green shirts and half are given orange, the people wearing green will start to think green is best.

This happens even among small children. In 2011, a psychology professor named Yarrow Dunham and his team gave green or orange shirts to kindergartners. They then showed those kids pictures of possible playmates wearing green or orange. "Which of these kids look nice?" they asked. Kindergartners overwhelmingly liked their own gender best. Girls gave more points to girls, and boys to boys. But they also liked their own color best.

Next, researchers gave the kindergartners a handful of coins and said, "Please divide the coins between the kids in these pictures." The green group gave a few more coins to green-wearers, and the orange to orange. And when asked to choose another kid to play with, kids in green shirts chose green-wearing friends.

It takes only tiny details to make us lump people into categories. And, of course, whichever category we happen to land in is always best. We're the heroes of our own minds.

It doesn't take much to make us feel part of a team. One study showed that people were more likely to cooperate if they shared a birthday. Another study found that people whose last names started with the same letter were more likely to get married!

Kids who have a
genetic disorder
called Williams
Syndrome don't
experience social
fear. They're
extra-friendly
to everyone.
These kids don't
stereotype based
on race. But they
do still group
people based on
gender. That proves
to scientists that
the way we sort
male and female is
different — inside
our brains — from
the way we sort
skin color.

Judgment Junction

Have you ever plopped a bowl on your head and worn it to school? Have you ever eaten cereal from your hat?

Probably not! We classify bowls as kitchen stuff and hats as clothing. We also recognize trumpets as musical instruments, daffodils as flowers and bees as insects. Our brains are bursting with categories.

For a long time, scientists wondered whether we sort people the same way we sort clothing, instruments and insects. But there was no way of knowing. At least, not until recent decades, when researchers began mapping the human mind and tracking brain waves and nerve activity.

In 2012, Boston scientists hooked up people to MRI scanners to create magnetic images of their brain activity. They asked their study participants to sort *objects*, and two areas of the brain — the frontal lobe and a spot near the base — lit up in the scans.

They then asked their subjects to sort *people*. Entirely different regions lit up.

Thanks to those Boston scientists, we now know that people-categories use many more regions of the brain than object-categories, including areas that handle social knowledge. When you see a pair of rain boots, you might think of outdoor clothing. But if you see Taylor Swift wearing those rain boots on a city street, your brain practically explodes with categories. You might think: *woman, singer, star — autograph! Should I ask, or shouldn't I?* You apply all sorts of stereotypes and weigh a wide variety of social cues to help you decide.

(Would *you* ask for her autograph?)

Baby Bias

Are we born this way, or do we learn our prejudices? The answer isn't exactly "black or white."

Yair Bar-Haim is a professor of psychology and neuroscience at Tel Aviv University in Israel. In 2006, he published a research paper about how babies react to faces. There were three groups of babies in his study:

- white babies living with white families in Israel
- black babies living with black families in Ethiopia
- black babies living in Israel in an immigration center, surrounded by caregivers and workers with various skin tones

Yair showed each baby two faces — one white and one black. The white babies looked much longer at white faces. The black babies living in Ethiopia looked longer at black faces. But the black babies living in the immigration center, the ones who were surrounded by both white and black people each day, showed no preference.

What does all this mean? We're not born with racial preferences or stereotypes, but we're definitely born with the capacity to learn them. We absorb them from our environments long before we understand what we're doing. The babies in Yair's experiment were only three months old!

This is partly why it's so difficult for people to unlearn stereotypes. We've been absorbing them since our baby days. Some of them are so ingrained, we don't even realize they exist.

Chapter 2

Secret Messages

Your mom says you can choose dinner tonight, so you sort through a stack of take-out menus. Chinese food, Greek, Thai, pizza ... you can't decide. Everything looks good.

Eventually, you make a list of pros and cons. When you're done, you can see that the Thai food is cheapest, quickest and most nutritious. But as soon as you pick up that menu, ready to show your mom, you feel a pang of disappointment. You realize you wanted pizza all along!

Sometimes, your rational mind knows what's best, but your unconscious mind thinks differently. In scientific terms, this is called dissociation. It means that two different parts of the brain can believe different things, without you realizing you have a conflict.

It's also one way that scientists explain a major mystery: how people can *know* that all humans are equal but still *act* with bias. It turns out that stereotypes and prejudice don't live in our rational, list-making minds. They live deeper, way down where the pizza cravings hide.

Hello, Ralph's Garage?

Are you a racist? Check yes or no.

By the 1950s and '60s, most people in North America checked "no" on questionnaires. They knew that racism is wrong. But researchers could still see discrimination happening around them. So what was going on? How could there be racism without racists?

One thing was clear: the old way of measuring these things — with surveys and questionnaires — wasn't working anymore. In 1971, psychologists Samuel Gaertner and Leonard Bickman set out to find a new method. They needed a better way to determine whether racism existed in the real world.

They set up a series of "wrong number" calls. Either a black actor using a Southern accent or a white actor using a New York accent would say the following lines: "Hello, Ralph's Garage? This is George Williams ... Listen, I'm stuck out here on the parkway ... and I'm wondering if you'd be able to come out here and take a look at my car?"

Of course, the person who answered the phone would say something like, "I'm sorry, this isn't Ralph's Garage. You have the wrong number."

"This isn't Ralph's Garage! Listen, I'm terribly sorry to have disturbed you, but listen ... I'm stuck out here on the highway ... and that was the last dime I had! I have bills in my pocket but no more change to make another phone call ... Now I'm really stuck out here. What am I going to do now?"

Of course, this was long before the time of cell phones. The caller was stranded at a pay phone with no change. So, would the person who answered this "wrong number" call make an effort to help the stranded stranger?

Samuel and Leonard found that people were very good at detecting whether callers were black or white. In separate tests, listeners judged white callers as white and black callers as black with more than 90 percent accuracy.

They also found that people discriminated. White people helped white callers 12 percent more often. The researchers called this "a small but detectable influence."

Experiments like this one were repeated throughout the United States. Researchers left college application letters in phone booths (with a white student photo or a black student photo) to see if strangers would be kind enough to mail them. They dropped boxes of pencils, asked for Salvation Army donations and staged falls on subway cars, all to see if white people would help white people more often than black. And they did.

When surveys asked Americans if they were racist, Americans said no. But in real-world situations, people's behavior still showed bias.

Nothing to See Here

When you meet someone, do you mention that you fart in your sleep? Or maybe you say, "Hello. Nice to meet you. Sometimes, when a sneeze catches me by surprise, snot flies out of my nose."

Probably not!

You keep those facts hidden away, and you focus on making a good impression. Depending on the person you're meeting — a potential friend, a new teacher, the town mayor — you might choose to reveal and hide different things. That's normal. It's one of the ways we humans try to fit in with those around us.

Imagine your life as a theater. The people nearby are the audience. They see your stage, where you present yourself to the world. But you also have a backstage, where you do your thinking and keep your secrets.

The difference between the stage and the backstage is what researchers call impression management. That term was coined by a Canadian-born professor named Erving Goffman in the 1950s. Basically, it means that we try to hide our flaws and present our best face to the world. We talk about fashion instead of sleep farts, and sunshine instead of snot.

Having both a stage and a backstage helps everyone get along. It certainly helps avoid embarrassing situations. But it also makes it more difficult for scientists to figure out how discrimination happens.

Impression management was the reason American researchers in the 1960s and '70s found it so tricky to measure racism. By then, everyone knew that racism is wrong. So if they had biased thoughts, they hid them. But that didn't mean they treated everyone equally in real life.

Decades later, we're all still hiding our biased thoughts.

Brain Bugs

In the 1990s, professors Anthony Greenwald and Mahzarin Banaji were working on psychology projects together, along with a graduate student named Brian Nosek. One day, Mahzarin sat down to take a draft version of a new test. It asked her to sort out words like *career* and *family*, interspersed with male and female names.

When she was asked to put male names and work-related words into the same category, Mahzarin was quick. When she tried to sort female names and work words into one category, she was slower.

Something's wrong with this stupid test, Mahzarin thought.

But it wasn't the test. Even though Mahzarin was a woman with a successful academic career, the test had revealed a bias deep in her brain. Somewhere among her neurons lived the belief that work should be more closely associated with men. That belief existed without Mahzarin's conscious knowledge.

Remember the Thai food and the pizza, and how your brain might know that Thai is more healthy, but your inner self craved pizza? Mahzarin's brain was playing the same sort of trick. She knew that women were just as capable of having careers. But somewhere deep in her pizza brain, in a place she couldn't consciously access, she held a men = work stereotype.

Together, Mahzarin and her colleagues, Anthony and Brian, began to develop more of these awkward sorting tasks. They created the Implicit Association Test (IAT). *Implicit* means something that exists but isn't obvious. And that's what the professors thought was happening with things like sexism and racism. They were hidden inside people's minds, in almost invisible forms.

Today, the IAT is used by researchers and regular people all over the world. The most famous version asks people to sort white and black faces into categories with positive and negative words. Most people who take the test find it easier to group white faces with positive words. Their fingers move more slowly when they try to group black faces with positive and white with negative.

Mahzarin and Anthony call this a "mind bug." It's like a glitch in a computer system, except it happens inside our brains. The results can be shocking, especially for people who think they fully support ethnic diversity or gender equality.

Activists, journalists, professors, researchers, police officers and ordinary citizens have all shown bias on the IAT. Almost three-quarters of people are faster when they link white with good than they are when they link black with good. Even most black people are quicker with the white = good link. It turns out that most of us have implicit biases of one sort or another, absorbed from the world around us.

Over the past few decades, Mahzarin and Anthony have used the IAT to show bias toward attractive people, toward heterosexual people and toward men. And Americans aren't the only ones to discriminate. In Japan, people assume those who use the Osaka dialect are less intelligent. Australians show implicit bias against people of Asian descent. Swedish people show bias against Muslims.

"Bias" in Swedish is *partiskhet*. But it's just as concerning in any language.

If It Quacks Like a Duck …

Some researchers have argued that the IAT doesn't reflect real-world actions. Just because you flunk an association test doesn't mean you're a racist. This might be true. But follow-up studies have found that cities where lots of people fail the test are the same cities where there's more violence against minorities. And one mega-study looked at 184 research projects and concluded the IAT *did* predict racist behavior.

The Bullet Bias

In April 2017, police in Balch Springs, Texas, received a 911 complaint. There were teens at a house party, said the caller, and they were drinking. Police arrived, entered the house and told everyone to go home.

Then they heard gunshots.

Officer Roy Oliver raced outside, where a car was driving away. Roy shot three times into the passenger-side window. He killed a black fifteen-year-old named Jordan Edwards.

Jordan was unarmed, and police later confirmed there were no weapons inside the car.

Roy was quickly suspended from the police force. In 2018, he was sentenced to fifteen years in prison. But that didn't answer all the questions about this case. Did the officers really hear gunshots? The police said the car was reversing toward them, but video footage showed the car was driving away. Were the police lying, or mistaken? What made Roy shoot?

We'll probably never know the answers to these questions. We might not get answers to similar questions about the 222 other black people shot by police in the United States in 2017. (African Americans make up 13 percent of the country's population, but they account for almost a quarter of police shootings.)

You can take the IAT yourself. It's online at Project Implicit: https://implicit.harvard.edu/implicit/ If you'd like to try Joshua Correll's video game, go to his website: http://psych.colorado.edu/~jclab/FPST/demo/canvas/testPrograms/st_v.l.html

We may not get answers, but scientists have some educated guesses. A University of Colorado professor named Joshua Correll has helped design a video game to illustrate the issue. As video games go, it's fairly tame. There are no fancy sound effects and zero animation. All the game does is flash a series of photos. Then a man appears. He's holding either a gun or a harmless object such as a cell phone. The player's job is to shoot the gun-toting bad guys but not the phone-holding good guys.

Joshua has invited hundreds of people to play his video game. Again and again, they show bias. They're quicker to shoot armed black men than armed white men. They're faster to press the "don't shoot" button for unarmed white men than they are for unarmed black men. Somehow, the stereotypes inside their brains are whispering: "Black men are dangerous. Shoot quick!"

Joshua believes that our stereotypes actually change the way our brains interpret visual information. Imagine your decision-making process as a teeter-totter. "Gun" sits on one end of the teeter-totter and "cell phone" on the other. Your brain is the fulcrum, the point where everything's balanced.

Joshua's research suggests that when the photo shows a white man, the fulcrum (your brain) shifts a tiny bit further toward "cell phone." When your eyes examine the man and send the visual clues to your brain, your brain's already a tad on the cell phone side. That makes it easier to hold your fire.

When the photo shows a black man, your fulcrum shifts a bit toward "gun." The stereotypes in your brain have moved the middle of the teeter-totter toward the dangerous side. So if your eyes spot a gun, your brain is already partway there.

Trigger Talk

In Canada, twenty-nine people were shot and killed by police in 2017. Four were black; six were Indigenous. Both of those numbers are high because black people and Indigenous people are small minorities of the population (2.5 percent and 4.3 percent).

But most developed countries have far fewer police shootings than the United States, probably because of stronger gun control. In Britain, police shot five people between January and July 2017, four of them related to terrorist attacks. In Australia, police shootings average about five per year. In Germany, they average about ten. In Japan, officers spend more time training in martial arts than they do on target practice, and shootings are extremely rare. In Norway, Iceland and New Zealand, police don't even carry guns.

Split Decisions

After years of experimenting with his video game, Joshua wondered if police officers would respond the same way as regular people. Police officers are experts, highly trained in split-second decision-making. They're constantly responding to threats. Would they be better at keeping their mental teeter-totters balanced?

Joshua and his team tested 127 police officers from Denver, Colorado, and another 113 officers from police departments across the United States. They found that officers were much better than regular people at making quick, correct decisions. They were also more fair. They showed no bias in the number of armed black men and armed white men they "shot."

But that didn't mean the police officers were free from stereotypes. Their biases still showed in the speed of their decisions. They were faster at shooting armed black men than armed white men, and faster to choose not to shoot unarmed white men.

The conclusion? Police officers hold stereotypes, just like the rest of us. But their training and practice help them fight against those stereotypes when making judgments.

But wait ... that doesn't explain why unarmed black men are shot more often than unarmed white men. What's up?

Researchers suggest that while police officers perform well in the lab, the real world is different. In the middle of a typical night shift, officers are sleep deprived. They're often in high-adrenaline situations, their bodies jittery from stress. All of these things might make them more vulnerable to stereotypes and bad decision-making.

Not all police officers who shoot unarmed black people are racists. But, just like the rest of us, they're influenced by stereotypes. And because they're carrying weapons, those stereotypes can be deadly.

So, how can we prevent wrongful shootings? How can we kick stereotypes out of the decision-making process? Fortunately, scientists are doing a lot of research and testing all sorts of new methods. You'll read more about this in Chapter Five.

First-Grade Brain Drain

Girls or boys: Who's smarter?

Five-year-old girls think girls are particularly brilliant, and five-year-old boys think boys are geniuses. But when those kids turn six, things start to change. Suddenly, both boys and girls think boys are more likely to be "really, really smart," and girls begin to avoid games and activities designed for super-smart kids.

That's what American researchers found in 2017. The results were the same, even when the girls got better grades in school. They still thought the boys were more brilliant!

Those six-year-olds had learned a stereotype. And just as the black = dangerous stereotype might lead to more police shootings of unarmed black men, the boys = brilliant stereotype can lead to discrimination against girls. Here are a few of the grown-up results of this particular bias:

- An American study showed that business ideas pitched by men are more likely to get investor support than ideas pitched by women. (If the men are good-looking, they get even more money.)

- In Belgium, researchers proved that female politicians get less media coverage than male politicians. Men are mentioned more often and given more time to speak.

- In the United States, Britain and Australia, scientists analyzed newspaper sports sections. Only 3 percent of the stories showcased female athletes.

- Canadian scientists found that even though female engineers publish in more respected journals, their research is used and mentioned less often than the work of male engineers.

We begin sorting by gender when babies are still wearing sleepers — blue sleepers with dinosaurs for boys, and pink sleepers with kittens for girls. We learn stronger stereotypes in elementary school, and those biases follow us all the way to the grown-up world. But not all dinosaurs were male, not all kittens are female — and not all gender stereotypes make any sense at all.

Sexism for Sweethearts

Like racism, sexism has become more subtle over time. Most people no longer admit to thinking men are better scientists, teachers or politicians. Now, they practice something researchers call benevolent sexism. That's like saying "friendly sexism." It means thinking women are sweet, nurturing or in need of rescue or protection. But, friendly sounding or not, it skews beliefs and achievements.

Researchers in Belgium set up a series of fake job interviews. In some, the employers said they were being forced to hire a certain percentage of women, even though women were weaker. They said, "I hope women here won't be offended; they sometimes get so easily upset! You'll work with men only, but don't believe what those feminists are saying on TV; they probably exaggerate women's situation in the industry simply to get more favors!"

That was outright, hostile sexism. Women noticed it right away.

In other interviews, the fake employers said they would choose women over men when all other qualifications were equal.

> Sexism can be harmful for boys, too, especially if those boys don't match the swashbuckling, knight-in-shining-armor stereotype.

They added, "You'll work with men only, but don't worry, they will cooperate and help you to get used to the job. They know that the new employee could be a woman, and they agreed to give you time and help."

That second example sounds much friendlier. Far fewer of the women candidates noticed any sexism or felt angry after hearing those words. But look at those sentences closely. While they're not hostile, they do imply women are weaker and will need more help.

And here's the shocker: when asked to write a job-skills test, the women exposed to the benevolent sexism scored lower than the women exposed to hostile sexism. The friendly "we'll take care of you" speech actually made things worse!

What was going on? All of the candidates said they felt motivated to perform their best. They all tried hard. But the women in the benevolent situation, even though they didn't see sexism, said they felt uncomfortable. The interview was unpleasant. And when the researchers did more experiments, they found three things that affected women's performance: preoccupation, self-doubt and self-esteem. At some level, those women were thinking, "If I need help to do this job, maybe I'm not good enough."

Benevolent sexism can be more damaging than it seems.

Pretty Crazy

In 2015, a technology company in San Francisco launched a recruiting campaign that featured photos of its workers, including an engineer named Isis Wenger. Some people thought the photos were fake; they said Isis was too pretty to be a real engineer. Soon, an #iLookLikeAnEngineer campaign went viral on Twitter, as diverse people posted their photos to prove that looks and engineering talent aren't related.

All the Pretty People

Did you fall straight from heaven? Because you look like an angel.

That's a cheesy pickup line. But science shows we're all a bit biased toward people who look like angels. Researchers call it an attractiveness halo. When we spot someone who's particularly pretty, we expect that person to be good, too.

- Researchers at Harvard asked four- and five-year-olds to choose the most trustworthy people. The kids thought good-looking people were more truthful, even if those people had lied to them in the past.
- When kids are attractive, teachers believe them to be smarter, more social, more confident and more popular.
- In mock trials, overweight women were more likely to be found guilty.

But it's not all good news for pretty people. The beauty bias can backfire. In Britain, researchers showed people pictures of students who were accused of plagiarizing and cheating. When the offense was minor, pretty people received the same punishments as others. But when the offense was major, they received extra punishment! Researchers suggested that we hold attractive people to a higher standard. Pretty is supposed to equal good. The angels in the experiment had tarnished their halos.

good-looking SOCIAL ATTRACTIVE CONFIDENT smart popular popular TRUTHFUL UNTRUSTWORTHY BAD guilty UNTRUSTWORTHY pretty LIAR

What's Up, Doc?

In 2004, a forty-five-year-old Indigenous man named Brian Sinclair wheeled himself into a Winnipeg emergency room. He was a double amputee with a urinary tract infection.

For more than a day, Brian sat slumped in his wheelchair in the waiting room. Four separate strangers approached hospital staff members to voice concerns about Brian. Still, he was ignored. When doctors and nurses walked by, they saw an Indigenous man, probably homeless. They assumed he was drunk, or he'd already been discharged, or he was trying to escape the cold weather outside.

Was the hospital staffed by racists? The doctors and nurses would likely say no! But they made assumptions without talking to Brian or examining him. They jumped to conclusions based on stereotypes deep in their minds.

Thirty-four hours after he arrived, Brian died in the emergency room.

A group of doctors and professors formed the Brian Sinclair Working Group to figure out what had gone wrong. After years of study, they released a report that argued Brian was killed by racism. Hospital staff had seen an Indigenous man and assumed he was drunk, not sick.

Implicit bias — judgments that doctors and nurses don't even realize they're making — leads to other sorts of medical errors, too. Studies have shown that American emergency-room doctors give blood-clot therapy less often to black patients. Women having heart attacks are more likely to be misdiagnosed. LGBTQ+ people are less likely to get good care.

Discrimination can be as simple as body language. Doctors who feel bias against certain patients might lean away from them or make less eye contact. Even when patients don't consciously recognize the bias, they feel it. They might ask fewer questions or return to the doctor's office less often.

Just like police officers, doctors are human. They fall prey to the same biases we all do. But everyone deserves great medical care. Today, activists and researchers are working hard to make sure all patients are treated fairly, whether or not they're part of minority groups. You'll read more about these efforts in Chapter Five.

What Rhymes with Race?

Do you remember *The Cat in the Hat*? That book was written by Theodor Seuss Geisel, better known as Dr. Seuss. Before his death in 1991, he published more than sixty books for children, and it's easy to remember his rhymes.

But recently, people have been looking at books like *The Cat in the Hat* and *Happy Birthday to You!* in new ways. They've noticed that 98 percent of his picture book characters are white. Illustrations that show people of color sometimes portray them as ridiculous stereotypes — a man who looks Middle Eastern wearing a tasseled hat and riding a camel, for example.

Was Dr. Seuss a racist? Maybe. Early in his career, he drew political cartoons that were downright offensive. (It was also a time when racism was much more common and more acceptable than it is now.) On the other hand, Dr. Seuss wrote entire books about treating people equally and not picking on those who are different.

Whether or not he did it on purpose, Dr. Seuss included a lot of racial stereotypes in his illustrations. And today, small readers might find "truer than true" representations of themselves in other, more diverse books.

In 2014, children's authors Ellen Oh and Malinda Lo found themselves at a book conference, listening to an all-white, all-male panel. Why were so many panels like this? they wondered. North American readers had changed. Shouldn't publishers change, too? Readers needed children's books featuring gender diversity, people with disabilities and people of color. Ellen and Malinda tweeted their thoughts, using the hashtag #WeNeedDiverseBooks.

Their messages quickly went viral. Eventually, that led to an international campaign. Today, We Need Diverse Books is a nonprofit organization with thousands of supporters around the world, working to promote changes in the publishing industry.

Meanwhile, other activists are working to change children's cartoons, video games, toy marketing and more. Kids between the ages of two and eleven see 25 600 ads per year. About 80 percent of North American ads show white people. In toy ads, boys play with guns and girls play with dolls. Is it any wonder we absorb stereotypes as we grow?

Stereotypes are strengthened by media coverage, advertising and government policies. Sometimes, we even strengthen them ourselves ...

Chapter 3

Me, Myself and I

The in-crowd versus the outsiders. The rich versus the poor. The athletes versus the computer geeks. We categorize each other every day, both intentionally and by accident. But here's the crazy part: we also categorize ourselves!

Studies have shown that Asian girls do better on math tests if they're subtly reminded of their Asian identity. Senior citizens score poorly on IQ tests if they're reminded of their age. First-graders from disadvantaged families score worse than those from rich families if they're told their intelligence is being measured and compared.

Because stereotypes have seeped into our brains, we can't help applying those assumptions to our own lives. That, in turn, can affect our behaviors.

To change the way we judge the world, we might first have to change how we judge ourselves.

Mirror, Mirror

How much information are you sharing with the world? Take a look at your outfit. Are you wearing anything from this list?

- a dress or skirt
- piercings
- hair accessories
- a sports watch
- a ball cap
- braids
- dreadlocks
- a cross, yarmulke or hijab
- expensive brand names

By wearing any of these items or styles, you broadcast messages about your identity. For example, picture a tall kid with close-cropped hair wearing expensive sneakers, nylon shorts and a basketball jersey with a team name emblazoned across it. Are you picturing a boy or a girl right now? Do you imagine a specific ethnicity? And what do you think that person likes to do?

What if you spot an Asian kid with wire glasses and long, straight hair carrying a violin case?

Hey! What do you mean she's a musical prodigy? That's a total stereotype, and you don't even know the person. It could be a guy. He *could* be a huge basketball fan ... but that probably wasn't your first guess.

We sort people by gender, ethnicity, religion, political views and social status — all with a single glance. Every day, strangers make assumptions about us based on stereotypes. And every day, we help them do it. We choose gender-specific clothing, haircuts and jewelry. We broadcast information through brand names, T-shirt slogans and hat choices.

Categorizing ourselves makes life easier. If you're a biker, it's easier to spot other bikers when they're wearing leather jackets and have tattoos. What a pain if you had to stop everyone on the street and say, "Hey, do you like motorcycles? Want to hang out later?"

Take a look at what you're wearing right now and search for identity clues. Sometimes, our clothing choices send powerful messages.

Power Suits

Mahatma Gandhi was a political activist, protesting Britain's rule over India. In 1921, he abandoned his formal clothing and began wearing the simple cotton loincloth of a peasant. Gandhi was sending two messages:

- He represented all classes, not only rich people who could afford fancy clothes.
- Britain wasn't best! India should reclaim its own traditions, including hand-woven cotton.

When a journalist asked how he felt wearing such simple clothing while meeting the King of England, Gandhi said, "There was no problem. His Majesty more than made up for both of us."

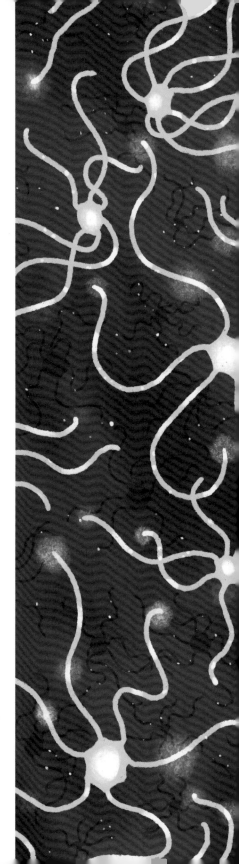

The Civil Rights Movement didn't win equal access in time for Claude to attend a different high school. In fact, many say the fight was never won; Chicago schools remain highly segregated today.

Nerves of Steele

As a kid in Chicago in the early 1950s, Claude Steele was allowed to swim only on Wednesday afternoons. All the other afternoons were reserved for white kids.

He remembers learning that rule; it was the first time he realized he was black. And the pool wasn't the only problem. In his city, black kids went to black schools in black neighborhoods. White kids went to white schools in white neighborhoods. And the school superintendent, Benjamin Willis, thought this was just perfect. Kids should go to school in their own communities, he said.

The Civil Rights Movement thought otherwise. The white kids had better buildings, smaller class sizes and more funding. They had empty desks available. Meanwhile, black kids were stuck in portable classrooms and overcrowded buildings.

Claude, along with his dad and brothers, joined thousands of other protesters at rallies and marches, demanding integrated schools and equal education for all.

All of this came back to Claude when, during his first year of university, he saw a black psychologist on the news talking about people's motivations during a race riot. The man was clear, confident and insightful. Claude was so impressed, he abandoned all thoughts of a dentistry career. He signed up for psychology courses, enrolled in graduate school and began leading his own research projects.

Eventually, he became a psychology professor at Stanford University. He wrote a bestselling book called *Whistling Vivaldi: And Other Clues to How Stereotypes Affect Us*. And he became famous for a particular idea: stereotype threat.

The Invisible Balloon

Stereotype threat: knowing someone believes bad things about you, and worrying you're going to confirm those beliefs.

Because we all recognize stereotypes — even the ones that apply to our own groups — we carry them with us. Claude describes stereotypes like balloons, always bobbing along above our heads. In certain situations, those balloons change the way we act.

Imagine a girl in a room full of boys, preparing to write an algebra exam. The balloon above her head says "girls ≠ math." She knows everyone else believes that balloon. And because she feels judged, she doesn't do as well as she normally would on the math problems.

Stereotype threat is different than self-doubt or insecurity. We can usually recognize those things in ourselves and work to overcome them. Stereotype threat is something more subtle, and it happens in more specific situations.

When two people are talking, they're having one conversation out loud. Under the surface, their body language and subconscious minds are having an entirely separate conversation. And if one person's subconscious feels judged, it reacts — without necessarily notifying the conscious brain.

Through years of experiments, Claude and his colleagues discovered that stereotype threat hurts people's performance at work, on sports fields and, in particular, at school. It isn't the *only* problem for black kids in school, Claude argues, but they'll never have an equal chance until it's recognized.

Making the Grade

In one of Claude's early stereotype-threat experiments, he asked both black and white students to write a test. He told one group that it was an intelligence test, but he didn't mention this to the other group.

Black students did better on the no-instructions version and worse when they thought they were taking an intelligence test. Claude suggested this was because of stereotype threat. The students had absorbed the idea that white kids are smarter than black kids. They became nervous about upholding that stereotype, and their anxiety affected their test scores.

Tests aren't the only problem. Before people take math tests, they have to learn math. And stereotype threat can affect early learning.

In 2017, researchers gathered a group of 135 American fifth-grade students who were studying ratios. The students were black or members of other minority groups. First, the students were asked to write a test to evaluate their skill level. A few days later, they were asked to watch a lesson about ratios. But before the lesson began, half the students were asked to write the date; the other half were asked to write down their race. The rest of the lesson was exactly the same.

When researchers visited a third time, the following week, they asked students to write a test to show how much they had learned from the ratios lesson. The ones who'd been asked to write down their race made more mistakes and remembered less. The ones who'd written the date remembered more and performed better. This applied to both struggling students and great students. A simple question about skin color had changed the way they learned.

Researchers have shown this type of stereotype threat at work in many scenarios:

- when poor people are told their intelligence is being measured against the intelligence of richer people
- when white athletes are told their natural skills are being compared to those of black athletes
- when old people are told their memory skills will be judged
- when girls are told their math abilities will be measured against those of boys

By changing the way they give instructions, researchers can change the stereotype threat felt by people in each of these groups — and change the way people perform.

True or False?

What if the stereotypes are true? What if girls are genetically wired for art, not algebra?

In one of Claude's early experiments, researchers gave students a difficult math test. One group was told that the results of the test often showed gender differences. The women of that group did poorly. But a second group was told, "On this *particular* test, women always do as well as men." Both the men and women in that group performed well! Researchers have also found that girls do best in math and science when they live in countries with fewer stereotypes.

Conclusion: girls and boys have equal algebra genes.

Name Games

There were about 100 000 Muslim people living in Sweden in the 1980s. Today, there are half a million people with Muslim heritage. As more immigrants and refugees arrive, that number continues to grow.

These new citizens face serious stereotypes. They often don't get the same job opportunities as those with Swedish-sounding names. Some Muslim immigrants have taken an unusual step to evade those stereotypes: they've changed their names.

The government forms required for a name change ask people why they're switching. Most people with traditional Muslim-sounding names give one of three reasons:

- Their names are too difficult for others to pronounce.
- Their names cause discrimination.
- They want to distance themselves from their ethnic community.

They're not imagining the discrimination. According to researchers, Muslim immigrants who have more Swedish-sounding names receive higher incomes, have better chances at job interviews and are treated with more gender equality. But our names are important parts of our identities, and changing them is an extreme choice. In an ideal world, people wouldn't have to adopt new labels to achieve equality.

Skin Deep

Remember the ways we broadcast information to others? Through our clothing, jewelry and haircuts? Our names — Swedish-sounding, Muslim or otherwise — are another of those ways. So are skin tones, scars and wrinkles.

In 2016, Americans spent US$16 billion on plastic surgery. In China, people spent more than US$100 billion. And if you're thinking, "I'd never do that," check your bathroom counter. See any makeup or lotion there? North Americans buy about US$90 billion of beauty products each year.

Plastic surgery and beauty products change our looks, and therefore change the information we send to others. When we broadcast information that's a bit misleading, we might prompt others to categorize us the way we'd like to be seen, instead of the way we really are. Usually, old people hope to be categorized as young, and young people hope to be categorized as older.

Sometimes people broadcast information to fit a minority stereotype. For example, researchers have tracked the way lesbians and gay men use clothing and jewelry to publicly identify themselves. Their outfits can create group identity *and* serve as political statements, all at the same time.

The Nerd Herd

Only one-fifth to one-third of computer programmers are women. That applies in countries all over the world, from Canada to Japan, South Korea to Germany. And in most developed countries, the number of girls enrolling in computer science has dropped in recent years. Girls don't even take the introductory courses — they say they're not interested.

What's going on?

One answer: the "nerd factor." When girls think of computer science, they probably think of geeky guys staring at computer screens, avoiding interaction with the outside world. They might imagine people who memorize Star Wars movies and play Dungeons and Dragons late into the night. In other words, girls hold a stereotype about programmers.

At the University of Washington, a professor named Sapna Cheryan had an idea. What if she could change that stereotype by adjusting the way computer labs looked? The computer science lab at her own university wasn't the usual male domain, full of action figures and energy drinks. And the lab *did* have more female students than most. Had the women come first, changing the space, or had the changed space attracted female students?

Sapna created two classrooms. One featured Star Trek posters, computer parts and science fiction books. The other had nature posters, neutral books and water bottles. Sapna invited students inside and asked them how interested they were in computer science and how well they thought they'd perform. Men said they'd do equally well in either room, but most women far preferred the neutral environment. Even when female students were simply asked to *imagine* different computer labs, the ones picturing a more neutral lab felt more positive about programming.

Sapna's experiments suggest that computer science programs might attract more women simply by making their classrooms a little less masculine. She calls this "ambient belonging." It's the feeling you get when you walk into a room and believe you could fit in there.

Game Changers

There's one great thing about stereotype threat: it's easy to change. At least temporarily. Tiny hints and cues can make people feel more comfortable, shed their stereotype worries and perform better. In one experiment, black college students were told to think of intelligence as something that could change and grow over time. That one small suggestion improved their grades.

Claude Steele says the first antidote to stereotype threat is recognition. If people know it exists, they can be quicker to notice it happening and better able to control the situation.

Diversity is another solution. It's easy to feel stereotype threat if you're a tiny minority. One person with darker skin in a roomful of white people, or one girl in a roomful of boys, is bound to feel different. But if the room is full of people with all sorts of skin tones and gender identities, their differences become less important.

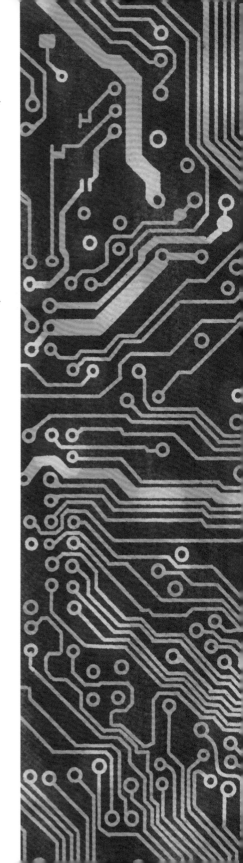

There are lots of other simple ways researchers have found to reduce stereotype threat. Here are a few things they suggest:

- Don't ask people about their age, gender or ethnicity at the beginning of a test. If you must ask those questions, put them on the last page.
- Encourage people to think of themselves as complicated, with a variety of skills, interests and abilities. Everyone has some in-group and some out-group qualities, and many that are unique. When we recognize that, we feel more comfortable in unfamiliar situations.
- Provide role models. When girls have more female math and science teachers, for example, they feel less stereotype threat.
- Focus on effort and motivation, not talent and genetics. We can't control our genes, but we can control our study habits.

There's another way to reduce stereotype threat: change society. Imagine if no one thought that white people were smarter, or boys were better at math, or old people were boring.

As humans, we can process vast amounts of information. What if we learned to use those abilities to think more complex thoughts about ourselves, our friends and family members, and even complete strangers? Ideally, we'd all take the time and make the mental effort to draw detailed pictures instead of relying on stereotypes.

There are whole movements of people working toward these goals. They don't want to change stereotype threat. They want to change the world.

Chapter 4

Change-Makers

In 1918, the *Ladies' Home Journal* gave this advice to mothers: "The generally accepted rule is pink for the boy and blue for the girl. The reason is that pink being a more decided and stronger color is more suitable for the boy, while blue, which is more delicate and dainty, is prettier for the girl."

What? Pink for boys and blue for girls?

Obviously, that stereotype changed over time. Two world wars made greens and browns more popular for "little soldiers" (boys). Clothing makers began selling more pink for girls and blue for boys in the 1940s. Then, the 1980s brought prenatal testing. Once parents knew in advance whether they were having a girl or a boy, pink and blue clothing sales skyrocketed.

All sorts of forces can affect our assumptions, from advertising to journalism and politics to protest movements. Sometimes, even a single person (read more about Mark Wellman on page 60) can help change a whole society's views.

Today, as protest groups march, movie stars strut and advertisers try (and sometimes fail) to set new standards, researchers are busy tracking the results. The answers aren't always black and white — or pink and blue, either.

Garlic Guesses

A garlic press. You stuff a clove of garlic inside, squeeze the handle and voila! Crushed garlic squishes from the top.

So ... if the press were a toy, would it be best for girls or for boys?

That's the somewhat ridiculous question that scientists asked preschool kids in 2017. Before they started the experiment, the researchers painted the garlic press. For some groups, they painted it pink. For others, they painted it blue.

"How much do you like this toy?" they asked the kids. "Who should play with this toy?"

Those little kids had no idea what a garlic press was or what it did. But the colors made a big difference. Girls were more interested in the pink press. And when the same researchers took traditional boy toys (model fighter jets, for example) and painted them pink, girls were more likely to want them. When they painted toy ponies black, blue and red, and gave them black manes, the ponies were suddenly considered boy toys.

Toys are some of the most gender-stereotyped items around. We buy dolls for girls and trucks for boys, fairy wands for girls and footballs for boys. Companies create ads showing girls baking cookies and boys sword fighting.

They even take the most simple of toys — things like building blocks — and market them separately to different genders.

Research shows that as kids get older, they're capable of replacing stereotypes with more complex and detailed decision-making methods. But toys don't always encourage this way of thinking. For decades, researchers, parents and activists have been asking companies to go more gender neutral. Boys should feel like it's normal to bake cookies. Girls need construction sets to boost their science and engineering skills. All kids should feel free to play with all toys.

So when Lego launched an entire line of pink and purple building blocks, that was a reason to celebrate. Or was it?

Building Blocks

In 2017, researchers studied the differences between Lego Friends kits, marketed to girls, and the more traditional Lego City kits. The differences they found went far beyond pink and purple bricks.

In the City kits, almost 90 percent of the miniature male characters had jobs. Kids could play with police officers, firefighters, doctors, astronauts, pilots and race car drivers. But in the kits designed for girls, only half the characters had jobs, and many of those were sales positions. Smoothies, lemonade or pizza, anyone?

There were other differences, too. In the Friends kits, a third of the characters did housework or cleaning. Boy characters in the City kits with similar chores? Zero.

Denmark, where Lego is made, ranks near the top of world lists for gender equality. Line Bonde became the nation's first female fighter pilot in 2006.

The researchers found that boy characters saved people from danger, while the girls lived in safe, idyllic settings. The boys were often experts ("No fire is too big!"). The girls were learning ("Practice until she's perfect then get ready at the pretty makeup table!").

So, did creating Lego Friends sets encourage girls to build their construction and engineering skills? Lego earned US$5.5 billion in 2017 and Friends kits were strong sellers — the company certainly found girl appeal. But it seems the marketing teams at Lego might have a little learning of their own to do.

Girls can be astronauts, too!

Easy Does It

In 2012, a thirteen-year-old girl named McKenna Pope made a YouTube video and launched a petition asking Hasbro to make an Easy-Bake Oven in gender-neutral colors. The version in stores was pink and purple and showed girls on the box. McKenna's four-year-old brother secretly wanted one, but he didn't want to ask for a girls' toy.

McKenna's video and her online petition went viral. She got 46 000 signatures in only a few weeks. Soon, Hasbro's directors called her up and invited her to their head offices, where they unveiled a black, blue and silver version of the toy oven.

Mission accomplished!

To hear more of McKenna's story, you can watch her TED Talk at www.ted.com.

Soaps to Save the World

A woman arrives at the front door of a neighborhood shop. She asks what has upset the young shopkeeper. She demands to be admitted. But the young shopkeeper doesn't want to let her in — she worries the woman will take her loved one to prison!

Does this all sound a little melodramatic? It's supposed to! This is a scene from *New Dawn*, a popular radio soap opera in Rwanda. It's a Romeo-and-Juliet story of two lovers from different villages trying to find a path between the distrust of their families and friends.

Real-life Rwanda has a violent past. In 1994, the Hutu ethnic group took over the government of Rwanda and prompted a mass slaughter. In just over three months, more than 800 000 members of the Tutsi ethnic group and their supporters were killed. The genocide left the country in shambles. Relations between the ethnic groups are still strained, more than twenty years later.

While the characters in *New Dawn* aren't identified as Hutu or Tutsi, they portray the story of people divided by distrust. That's no accident — the show was first funded in 2003 by a Dutch aid organization with the hope it might help unite the country. And it has.

When researcher Betsy Levy Paluck heard about the project, she flew from Princeton University to Rwanda to study the results. She found the show didn't necessarily change people's beliefs. They might still hold on to their ethnic distrust after listening to the stories. But it did change their behaviors. Fans of the soap opera were more likely to say they'd consider allowing their children to intermarry.

Betsy believes the show has helped people see a different version of normal, and perhaps a new vision for the future.

New Dawn isn't the only media project designed to challenge stereotypes. In Somalia, the United Nations (UN) sponsored a televised singing competition. They wanted to fight back against extremist groups who had once banned public song.

In 2018, the UN created a virtual reality film to show people what it's like to live as a Roma woman named Fatmira. Previously called "gypsies," Roma people face discrimination and prejudice across Europe. They're often considered thieves. But the UN hopes that when viewers virtually walk in Fatmira's shoes, stereotypes will change.

People Power

Crowds marching through city streets. People occupying government offices or chaining themselves to fences. Knitted pink hats, painted signs and drumbeats.

There are all sorts of massive movements designed to break down stereotypes and promote equality.

- Black Lives Matter was sparked in 2013 when a neighborhood watch coordinator shot Trayvon Martin, an unarmed seventeen-year-old boy in Florida. The movement has since spread across North America.

- Pride parades have promoted LGBTQ+ equality since 1970, when Chicago Gay Liberation organized a march through the city. That event took place a year after the Stonewall Riots, a series of demonstrations sparked by the police raid of a New York City gay bar. There are now thousands of annual Pride events around the world.

- In 2017, in response to the election of Donald Trump in the United States, the first Women's March drew close to five million people in the United States, and another two million in countries around the world. Participants rallied for a wide range of issues, including women's rights, immigration reforms, health-care reforms and racial equality.

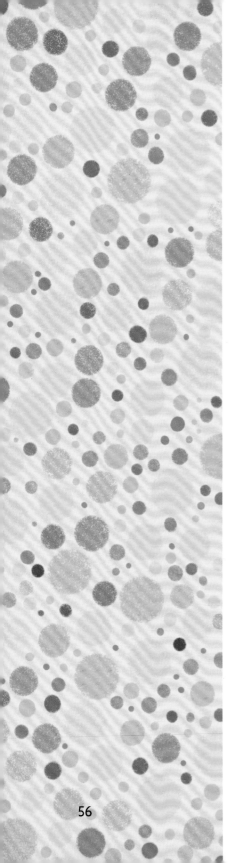

Events like these can force the attention of politicians, raise public awareness and draw new supporters. And when millions are marching, they *must* be changing stereotypes. Right?

Hmmm ...

There are major forces working *against* stereotype change. Media coverage sometimes portrays protesters as criminals, or focuses on property damage instead of delving into the reasons behind a demonstration.

There are also people who like the status quo. Have you ever heard someone say "all lives matter" in response to a Black Lives Matter protest? It might sound reasonable, at first. But Black Lives Matter is working for the rights of an underprivileged, stereotyped minority. "All lives" aren't facing serious stereotypes, so that argument misses the point.

Yet another problem: protests are usually one-day events. The next day, news coverage disappears, everyone heads back to work and school, and it's business (and discrimination) as usual.

Assumptions are tricky things, and it's hard for protesters to change the inner workings of the human brain. It's even harder for scientists to trace connections between specific events and stereotype change.

So, will Black Lives Matter overcome bias? Will Women's Marches close the gender gap? Not quickly. People have been fighting for racial and gender equality for hundreds of years, and the world still isn't perfect. But your neighborhood activist might argue that every few years we march a little closer.

Frame Games

You might frame a photograph. A piece of artwork. But can you frame a news story?

The news media is supposed to be objective. We need to hear both sides of every story. But by "framing," journalists are sometimes more friendly toward one side than another. (It's not always on purpose. Remember Chapter Two, about implicit bias? Journalists can accidentally discriminate, too.)

Next time there's a major protest, check out the news coverage.

- Does the news story focus on the problems that prompted the protest? Or does it talk about the event itself, the crowd and the police response? Often, journalists focus on the action. Ordinary viewers and readers don't necessarily learn about the background issues.

- Who gets interviewed? Sometimes all the attention goes to police representatives and politicians, instead of the protesters.

Not all news is bad news. Researchers studied the first Black Lives Matter events in 2014 and found that newspapers in New York and St. Louis framed the protests as peaceful and positive. It's possible that news coverage of minorities — and marchers — might slowly be changing.

Germ Warfare

Colds are contagious. Coughs are contagious. So are stereotypes.

Back in Chapter One, we discussed how authoritarian leaders see the world in black and white, or in-groups and out-groups, and prompt other people to do the same. That style of leadership didn't end with World War II.

Powerful leaders still set examples for others to follow. It's a process that scientists call affective contagion. If your school principal gives you a big smile as you pass in the hallway, you might feel a bit happier for the rest of your morning. But you might not realize why. When we're busy or distracted, we absorb these emotional transfers without even noticing.

That's a great thing when your smiling principal is transferring a good mood. But what if a politician is saying mean things about out-group minorities? That might transfer negative stereotypes. That's why scientists worry when European leaders rail against refugees, or U.S. President Donald Trump speaks out against Muslims. It's possible that ordinary citizens will hear those words and, without necessarily noticing, absorb negative stereotypes.

In January 2017, Alexandre Bissonette opened fire in a Quebec mosque. When police arrested and interviewed him, he said he'd been worrying about Canada's safety more and more after watching terrorist attacks on the news. U.S. President Donald Trump had announced travel restrictions to limit Muslim immigration, then Canadian Prime Minister Justin Trudeau said Canada would welcome immigrants and refugees.

Alexandre decided that, for the safety of his family, he needed to take action against Muslim immigrants. He told police: "They're going to kill my parents, my family, me, too. I had to do something."

That *something* had tragic results. Alexandre didn't kill terrorists. He killed six innocent men and seriously wounded others.

Was this a random act of violence? In the months after the attack, journalists and researchers suggested that stereotypes and affective contagion had played a role in the shooting. Of course, there's no way to know for sure. And there's much more research to be done on how stereotypes pass between people.

Marching Backward

Environmentalists have rallied. They've protested. They've chanted "Save the Bees" and started Meatless Mondays. So why isn't everyone on board? Why isn't the whole world driving electric cars, buying organic and going vegan?

It turns out there's a stereotype against ... activists! A 2013 study showed that people think of both feminists and environmentalists as eccentric, angry and even dirty. Those stereotypes reduce people's willingness to change.

Hand over Hand

El Capitan towers over Yosemite National Park, a granite cliff three times the height of the Empire State Building. Most climbers take three to five days to scale the monolith, spending nights in sleeping bags strapped to the rock.

Usually, those climbers use all four limbs.

Mark Wellman was a world-renowned climber who'd been scaling cliffs since he was a kid. He'd conquered the toughest routes on the Sierra Nevada peaks and the French Alps. But in 1982, a climbing accident left him paralyzed from the waist down.

But that didn't stop him. In 1989, he and his climbing partner, Mike Corbett, set out to ascend El Capitan. Mark rigged a special pull-up bar that allowed him to draw his body up the wall using only the strength of his arms. For him, tackling El Capitan is about the equivalent of doing 7000 pull-ups. (In his spare time, Mark sit-skied across the Sierra Nevada mountains, competed on the United States Disabled Ski Team and worked as a ranger at Yosemite.)

Mark's achievements helped prompt a whole new world of adaptive climbing equipment. People were soon using harness and pulley systems, specially designed pads and prosthetic climbing feet. The International Paralympic Committee recognized paraclimbing as an official sport in 2017.

Mark went from injured climber to innovative athlete, one pull-up at a time. He helped shift people's assumptions. But not all people with disabilities can do extreme sports, and they shouldn't have to.

Sometimes, society promotes a different sort of stereotype: if people with disabilities try hard enough, they can do the same things non-disabled folks can do. This is sometimes true, and sometimes not. People with disabilities can be powerful in their own ways, and they shouldn't have to climb mountains to prove it.

One other stereotype faced by people with disabilities? That they're courageous and need to overcome all barriers. Writer George Covington once said, "My disability isn't a burden; having to be so damned inspirational is."

Chapter 5

Rewiring the Mind

Wouldn't it be nice to flip open a control panel on your forehead, find the programming bugs that create bias, then type in a quick fix?

Unfortunately, we don't have control panels. Some of us haven't even recognized our need to de-bug. We absorbed our biases as babies and haven't stopped to think about them since. Those of us who belong to majority groups sometimes accept our privileges without considering the people who are left behind.

But, slowly, things are changing. Over the past two decades, researchers have begun to understand the ways prejudice and implicit bias work in the human brain. At the same time, campaigns against racial, gender and sexual discrimination have reminded us the world is not yet equal.

So how can we improve?

That's what millions of people are asking, all over the world. And that's the question scientists are now beginning to answer.

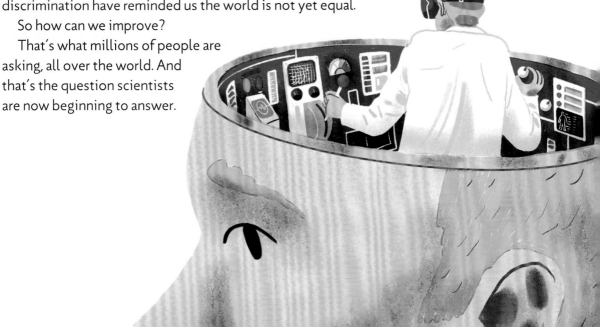

Cue the Violins

Good news! There's a solution to stereotyping. You simply carry around a cardboard box and place it over your head before meeting anyone new. That way, you avoid judging people based on their looks, ethnicity or gender.

What? Impractical, you say?

Well, the theory works just fine for symphony orchestras.

In 1969, double bassist Art Davis was playing for his local orchestra. He'd already won scholarships to the Juilliard School and the Manhattan School of Music. He was even appearing in TV productions. But when he asked to audition for the New York Philharmonic, they turned him away. Art Davis was black, and orchestra musicians were overwhelmingly white.

Art offered to audition from behind a screen so his talent could be blindly judged against the talent of other applicants. The orchestra again refused. That's when Art took the Philharmonic to court. He filed a lawsuit with the New York Human Rights Commission.

The commission said the orchestra's practices were almost certainly biased. Instead of hiring based on open auditions, they chose friends or took recommendations from current musicians. However, the Human Rights Commission said that artistic merit was difficult to judge, so they couldn't *prove* the orchestra had discriminated.

Art lost his lawsuit. He was so unhappy, he quit playing professionally for a decade.

But his voice hadn't gone unheard. And his idea of blind auditions, held behind screens, would eventually revolutionize orchestra hiring practices — not for people of color, but for women.

The typical American city orchestra includes about one hundred musicians. Until the 1980s, about 90 percent were male. Conductors argued that men were more musically talented than women.

In 1952, the Boston Symphony Orchestra had begun placing a screen between auditioning players and the hiring team, but it took another twenty years — and the attention garnered by Art's lawsuit — before other major orchestras followed Boston's lead.

Researchers have since pored over the hiring records of eight major American orchestras from the 1970s onward. They found that the use of screens prompted a 50 percent increase in the number of women who progressed from the initial auditions to the finals. Over time, those blind auditions led to a 25 percent increase in the number of female orchestra musicians.

Blind auditions haven't solved the diversity issue, though. In the United States, only about 4 percent of orchestra musicians are black or Latinx. In Britain, only 2 percent are from an ethnic minority. Apparently, screens aren't a quick fix for everything.

Along with a screen between musicians and listeners, orchestras had to provide a carpet to muffle the footsteps of the person auditioning. Otherwise, the sound of high heels sometimes gave women away!

Chineke!

The Chineke! Orchestra in Britain was the first in Europe to include mostly black and minority musicians. The group was founded by a double bass player named Chi-chi Nwanoku. In the middle of her career, she discovered a piece of music by a composer named Chevalier de Saint-Georges, the son of a French plantation owner and an enslaved woman. *Hey, she thought, there are black composers?* Suddenly, Chi-chi realized how little diversity existed in Britain's classical music scene.

Band programs had been cut from school budgets, so only middle-class white kids took lessons. Few kids were exposed to classical music, and fewer still saw a place on stage for minorities. Chi-chi set out to change all that with orchestra concerts, a nonprofit foundation and — most recently — a junior orchestra for teens.

White-Coat Conundrums

Remember the story of Brian Sinclair in Chapter Two? He was the Indigenous man who died in a Winnipeg hospital. Doctors and nurses had assumed he was drunk or trying to escape the cold.

There are all sorts of problems with stereotyping in hospitals and doctors' offices. Women are less likely to receive treatment for blood clots. Black people in the United States are less likely to receive painkillers. Without necessarily meaning to, doctors stereotype their patients, which in turn affects patient care.

But medical experts are scientists — they know how to research issues and solve problems. That's their specialty! So, all over the world, there are doctors working to stop stereotypes at the hospital doors. And they've found three main ways to counter discrimination.

The first is to better train staff. At many universities, medical students now learn about implicit bias. Sometimes, they even take the Implicit Association Test, which you read about in Chapter Two, in class. Then they practice techniques to clear their minds when seeing patients so they can avoid jumping to conclusions.

Another way to help? Train the patients. Obviously, bias isn't the fault of sick people. But if patients in emergency rooms can learn to recognize it, they can ask more questions and demand better care. Helping people recognize stereotype threat (remember Chapter Three?) can also help them stand up for themselves.

The third way to address discrimination is one of the most interesting: change the system. In an emergency room, that can be as simple as having nurses double-check patients in the waiting room to make sure no one's missed. (This is one of the ways Winnipeg hospitals revamped their standards after Brian's death.)

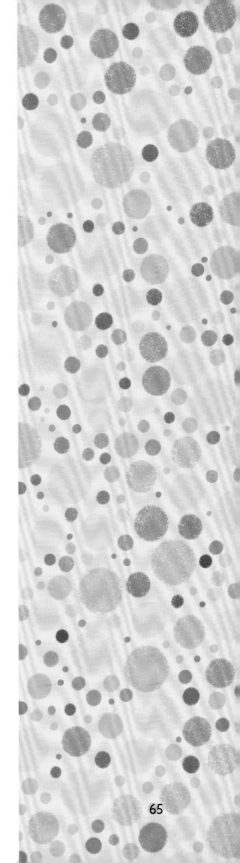

There are more detailed ways to counteract bias, too. In 2006, at Johns Hopkins Hospital in Baltimore, doctors realized that women weren't always receiving blood clot–busting medicines when they needed them. In fact, 45 percent of blood clots weren't getting diagnosed. The clots weren't as common in women, so doctors didn't always notice the warning signs.

Johns Hopkins designed a "decision support tool." Really, it's a checklist that pops up on the computer screen when a patient enters the ER. If a doctor or nurse checks the appropriate warning signs — *click, click, click* — the system suggests a treatment plan. And, unlike the human brain, the computer isn't pre-programmed for bias.

There are still lots of problems to solve when it comes to stereotypes in medicine. For example, almost all research has been done on small groups of doctors and patients. Most has focused on black patients in the United States. There are many more places and people who need a prescription to cure prejudice.

The Quick Fix

Parole denied!

If you're a judge, guess when you're most likely to make a snap decision and reject someone's parole application without giving it much thought. Guess when you're most likely to show bias in your decisions.

Right before lunch, when you're tired and hungry.

Maybe reducing bias is as simple as snack time!

Well, crackers and cheese probably won't solve all issues of prejudice and discrimination. But there *are* small efforts people can make to keep their decisions bias-free. The Implicit Association Test reveals hidden biases people don't realize they have. Researchers using that test have found a few simple things that can reduce bias scores.

Imagine

Creating a mental image of a strong woman, and spending a few minutes thinking about that woman, reduces gender bias.

Look Around

A 2001 study at New York University showed that looking at pictures of well-respected black Americans reduced race bias.

Meditate

A 2015 study showed that a few minutes of mindfulness can help people keep open minds.

Take Recess

Just like that parole-denying judge, we all need to give our brains a break sometimes. We make better decisions with full stomachs and clear minds.

These are all easy strategies we can use to make careful, conscious decisions instead of letting our inner biases take over.

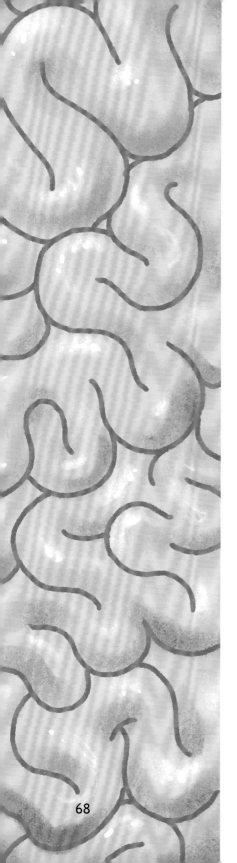

Unfortunately, the effects are temporary, and the methods aren't always practical. Imagine if you called 911, and the operator said, "A police officer will be right with you, as soon as she finishes her mindfulness break." Um ... that's not going to work!

Doctors can't stop an examination to imagine strong women every five minutes. Teachers can't take snack breaks before disciplining their students. So while these quick fixes are good, we still need more permanent ways to un-stick our stereotypes. As it turns out, scientists have just the thing ...

Meet and Greet

Remember Gordon Allport, the professor from Chapter One? Way back in 1954, when he published *The Nature of Prejudice*, he made a suggestion: if people hang out together as equals, they discover they have things in common. They learn that everyone's human. They grow less likely to stereotype.

Eventually, researchers took Gordon's guess and turned it into science. First, they gave it a fancy name: the contact hypothesis. Next, they designed experiments to see if it was true. They did more than 200 studies in twenty-five countries. They probed the biases and reactions of 90 000 people. What they found: 94 percent of the time, contact between groups reduced prejudice.

That's good news! We can all solve our own stereotyping problems ... *if* we're willing to hang out with people different than we are. That's the tricky part. We tend to like to spend time with people who are similar to us, instead.

When was the last time you had a sleepover and invited a bunch of weird people you didn't know? Probably never. That sounds like an uncomfortable experience! Now what if you were asked to have a sleepover not just with some strange kids from your school, but with enemies of your state? With people your family hated?

In Israel, Jewish people sometimes stereotype Palestinians as violent and dishonest. Meanwhile, Palestinians often think of Israeli Jews as violent, aggressive and inhumane. So imagine how Israeli and Palestinian kids feel each summer as they fly to the United States for the Seeds of Peace camp. Each year, the organization takes about 350 teens from conflict areas. Those kids get plopped in the middle of Maine to hike and canoe, with a side helping of conflict resolution. The idea is that by spending time together, on neutral ground, the campers will discover they have things in common. Then they'll return home with the leadership tools to help their ideas spread.

Does it work?

Well, the camp began in 1993, and the Middle East hasn't exactly achieved lasting peace since then. Some critics say that by focusing on *future* leaders and *future* goals, the organization makes peace seem impossible in the present. Others say that a few campers learning to shed their stereotypes will never be enough to sway entire communities. But researchers at the University of Chicago found that kids who attended the camp kept their new open-minded attitudes long after they returned home. And another study identified camp graduates helping with forty Middle East peace-building initiatives.

Who can tell what changes are yet to come?

What if there aren't any "different" friends in your classroom or on your soccer team? Researchers at Canada's McGill University found that reading books about friends who have different ethnicities can also help reduce prejudice.

Practice Makes Perfect

What if bias is a habit, like fingernail biting? Could we spread some of that foul-tasting anti-fingernail-biting goo on our biased brains and cure ourselves?

Patricia Devine at the University of Wisconsin thinks we can. Of course, it's a bit more complicated than fingernail goo. Patricia developed a seminar that trains people to recognize their own assumptions. Students are taught five strategies for avoiding bias. Though the strategies have fancy names, they're fairly basic concepts.

Stereotype Replacement
Recognize when you act based on stereotypes, figure out why and see if you can do better next time.

Counter-Stereotypical Imaging
Spend some time picturing successful black people, whether they're famous people, from the news or people from your neighborhood.

Individuation
Don't lump groups of people together. Think of everyone as unique.

Perspective Taking
Consider things from other points of view.

Increasing Opportunities for Contact
Hang out with people who are different.

People who took Patricia's course improved their scores on the IAT, and kept their scores better for at least two months after the course. She proved that when people are motivated to change, they can learn to recognize their biases, adjust them and hold on to their changed views over time.

Since her first experiments, Patricia has worked with police forces and other organizations across the United States to help bring her research results to the real world.

Stereotype Surprise

In 1914, a Canadian activist named Nellie McClung stood on stage at the Walker Theatre in Winnipeg. Before her, other women were arranged as if they were members of the government.

One woman proposed that men should have equal rights over their children.

How ridiculous, the other "government representatives" scoffed.

Another woman suggested that men should have a legal claim to property.

How silly!

Finally, a group suggested that men should be given the right to vote. The "premier," Nellie McClung, quickly turned them away.

"Politics unsettle men," she said, "and unsettled men mean unsettled bills — broken furniture, broken vows and — divorce."

The theater audience went wild with laughter because Nellie so closely imitated the real premier of Manitoba who, just the day before, had turned away a delegation of women seeking the right to vote. Flipping the gender roles suddenly made it clear just how ridiculous the premier's words had been.

Nellie's performance made the national news, and two years later, Manitoba became the first province to give women the right to vote.

Humor, satire and surprise can be useful weapons in the fight against stereotypes. Activists around the world have used them with powerful results. For example, Adam Fortunate Eagle, a Chippewa activist, once walked off a plane in Rome, Italy. He was in full traditional dress.

"In the name of the American Indian and pursuant to the Doctrine of Discovery," he declared, "I hereby lay claim to Discovery of Italy." He then planted a spear in the ground and called the country his own. It was September 24, 1973.

Of course, Adam didn't really want to *own* Italy. He wanted to show people how ridiculous it was to celebrate Christopher Columbus and his "discovery" of the Americas — lands already inhabited by Adam's ancestors.

Adam's stunt earned him front-page news headlines, a meeting with Italian President Giovanni Leone and even an interview with Pope Paul VI. He and the pope had a long chat about colonization.

With his bold, tongue-in-cheek move, Adam had drawn attention to the assumptions people made about discovery, about "uninhabited" lands and — especially — about Indigenous people.

Satire continues to make people aware of their assumptions, even today. Next time you watch *Saturday Night Live* or *The Daily Show*, watch how the comedians twist expectations to show just how ridiculous some of our stereotypes can be.

Culture Clash

Here's a good reason to shed stereotypes and embrace other cultures: it makes us more creative.

Adam Galinsky is a professor and researcher at Columbia University. He and his colleagues tracked international students and found that those who dated someone from another country became more creative. These students were more likely to start their own businesses when they returned home.

In 2009, Adam teamed up with a French professor named William Maddux to test the creativity of travelers. Then the pair looked at the creative powers of hundreds of people who were living in foreign countries. They found that travelers' abilities were average. But living abroad made them more creative problem solvers.

The researchers guessed that by having to adapt to a new culture and learn new ways of speaking and acting, people became better at looking at the world in new ways. Given a creativity problem, they'd automatically see it from more than one perspective.

Those new perspectives can be useful in other realms, too.

Many scientific studies are done by people from the same university, who share similar cultures and backgrounds. But a study by Harvard researchers Richard B. Freeman and Wei Huang found that when scientific studies involve researchers from different cultures, the results can be more powerful. They're used more often and credited more by other scientists.

Richard and Wei think there are two reasons for this: the cross-cultural blend gives researchers more creative ways to think about problems, and each author has a diverse group of followers and students, giving the research more of a following.

So, want to boost your creativity? Or your business smarts? Your scientific success? Simply hang out with people who are different than you are.

Tweetment

Prejudice in 280 characters or less: that's what an online platform such as Twitter can offer. Social media sites are rife with outright racism, and people often say things online that would never be acceptable in real life. This can leave minorities feeling vulnerable at their computer screens.

In 2017, a PhD student at New York University tested a tricky new way of taming racist slurs. Kevin Munger identified 231 Twitter users who had used the n-word in their posts. Then he created a series of fake accounts, or "bots," and made them look realistic by buying them each some followers.

When a racist used the n-word, Kevin had a bot send the person a message: "Hey man, just remember that there are real people who are hurt when you harass them with that kind of language."

If Kevin sent his reprimand from a bot with a profile photo of a black person, or from a bot with a white person's photo and few followers, there was no effect. But when the reprimanding tweet came from a white man with a lot of followers, the racists took notice. (Remember in Chapter One how much everyone wants to be part of the in-group? Kevin found a way to give the in-group higher standards, set by a member who seemed popular.)

When a racist tweeter received a rebuke from one of Kevin's white-guy, high-follower bots, the user's racist tweets dropped by 27 percent the following week, and remained lower in the future.

The Twitterverse is abuzz with possibilities.

~~Buyer~~ Advertiser Beware

In 2017, massive companies like PepsiCo, Walmart and Starbucks canceled their Google ads. The problem? People had noticed those ads playing on racist websites and YouTube channels. The consumer backlash was quick, and catastrophic for Google.

Suddenly, the company had a huge problem. It placed its ads based on math formulas, wherever they would receive the most attention. There was no easy, human-based way to make sure the ads remained on safe, non-offensive sites. Frantically, Google developed new tools to screen sites and videos for foul language and offensive content. The company promised advertisers more control over where ads would appear.

Were they successful? A few big advertisers returned, but so did the scandal. A 2018 CNN report found ads from 300 companies on YouTube channels promoting racism and pedophilia. Um ... oops?

A New Normal

We know that we like to be part of the in-group. We know that powerful leaders can shift the way we think. We know we're constantly, invisibly influenced by our society. All of that adds up to one conclusion: changing the world can change our brains.

In 1993, the Italian government passed a law reserving a percentage of city council seats for women. They wanted to encourage more women to run for leadership positions. But the law stayed in place for only two years. After that, the country's supreme court ruled against it.

The situation gave scientists a unique opportunity. During the two years under the law, some cities and towns had elected new councils. Others had not. So, had voting for women changed stereotypes and perceptions in some places? Yes! Researchers proved that being forced to vote for women in just one municipal election had changed the way that people acted. Years later, people in those towns were still voting for more female representatives, even though the law had long since gone.

What if all our leaders, in every country, spoke out against discrimination? What if countries everywhere passed laws ensuring equality for minorities?

In 1963, Dr. Martin Luther King, Jr. stood at a microphone in Washington, DC, and said, "I have a dream that one day this nation will rise up and live out the true meaning of its creed: 'We hold these truths to be self-evident, that all men are created equal.'"

Leaders like Dr. King can help change society. But so can those of us who aren't standing at a microphone.

The Chances for Change

The motivation method. It sounds like it might be a hot new exercise program. And it sort of is ... for the mind.

Most of the ways scientists have found to combat stereotypes have one thing in common: people must *want* to change. That means we need to notice prejudice and discrimination in the world around us. We need to recognize our own hidden biases. Once we know these things exist, we need to work for change.

Lots of that is already happening. Police officers in St. Louis, Missouri, are learning to recognize hidden bias. Hospitals are implementing new policies and procedures, like the one at Johns Hopkins, to ensure women get better blood clot–busting care. Soap opera producers in Rwanda are helping people develop empathy for other ethnic groups. In countries from Australia to Sweden, schools are teaching both students and teachers about bias.

There are also things we can do as individuals. Have you ever heard a racist joke or heard someone called a bad name? It's easy to stay silent or walk away. It's easy to feel powerless in that sort of situation. But there are definitely things we can do. Here are just a few:

Stand with the Victim
If someone's being called unkind names, you don't have to confront the name-caller directly. You can approach the victim, make eye contact and start a conversation. That lets the victim know you care and indirectly tells the aggressor that his or her words aren't appropriate.

Get Help
Sometimes, attacks keep happening because no one reports them. You can report harassing comments on social media sites, you can tell a teacher or principal about incidents at school or — in the case of a larger incident — you can call the police.

Get Involved

Volunteer for a refugee support agency, join a gender and sexuality alliance club at school, help your local librarian create a display of diverse books or offer to redecorate the computer lab.

Speak Up

Write to companies about biased products or ad campaigns, write to government representatives about laws to protect minorities or join a march for equality.

Expand Your Horizons

Remember the contact hypothesis? Through clubs, activities, sports games or classes, find ways to hang out with people who are different than you are.

Society doesn't suddenly, miraculously change. It takes millions of small steps to shift a stereotype. The good news? Small changes are easy. You probably made a few just by reading this book!

By using new knowledge and research, and by speaking out against prejudice, perhaps we can build a world in which children don't learn stereotypes with their ABCs.

Further Reading

Bausum, Ann. *The March against Fear.* Washington, DC: National Geographic Children's Books, 2017.

Bausum, Ann. *Stonewall: Breaking Out in the Fight for Gay Rights*. New York: Viking Books for Young Readers, 2015.

Jensen, Kelly, ed. *Here We Are: Feminism for the Real World*. Chapel Hill: Algonquin Young Readers, 2017.

Plous, Scott, ed. *Understanding Prejudice and Discrimination*. New York: McGraw-Hill Higher Education, 2013. http://www.understandingprejudice.org.

Scandiffio, Laura. *People Who Said No: Courage Against Oppression*. Toronto: Annick Press, 2012.

Smith, David J. *If the World Were a Village*. 2nd ed. Toronto: Kids Can Press, 2011.

Stevenson, Robin. *Pride: Celebrating Diversity & Community*. Victoria, BC: Orca Book Publishers, 2016.

Tate, Nikki. *Better Together: Creating Community in an Uncertain World.* Victoria, BC: Orca Book Publishers, 2018.

Tonatiuh, Duncan. *Separate Is Never Equal: Sylvia Mendez and Her Family's Fight for Desegregation*. New York: Abrams Books for Young Readers, 2014.

Selected Sources

Chapter 1

Bar-Haim, Yair, Talee Ziv, Dominique Lamy, and Richard M. Hodes. "Nature and Nurture in Own-Race Face Processing." *Psychological Science* 17, no. 2 (February 2006): 159–63.

Bottom, William P., and Dejun Tony Kong. "'The Casual Cruelty of Our Prejudices': On Walter Lippmann's Theory of Stereotype and Its 'Obliteration' in Psychology and Social Science." *Journal of the History of the Behavioral Sciences* 48, no. 4 (Fall 2012): 363–94.

Contreras, Juan Manuel, Mahzarin R. Banaji, and Jason P. Mitchell. "Dissociable Neural Correlates of Stereotypes and Other Forms of Semantic Knowledge." *Social Cognitive and Affective Neuroscience* 7, no. 7 (October 2012): 764–70.

Dunham, Yarrow, Andrew Scott Baron, and Susan Carey. "Consequences of 'Minimal' Group Affiliations in Children." *Child Development* 82, no. 3 (May/June 2011): 793–811.

Hecht, Jennifer Michael. "Vacher de Lapouge and the Rise of Nazi Science." *Journal of the History of Ideas* 61, no. 2 (April 2000): 285–304.

Katz, D., and K. W. Braly. "Racial Prejudice and Racial Stereotypes." *Journal of Abnormal Psychology* 30, no. 2 (July 1935): 175–93.

Schneider, David J. *The Psychology of Stereotyping*. New York: Guilford Press, 2003.

Stolier, Ryan M., and Jonathan B. Freeman. "Neural Pattern Similarity Reveals the Inherent Intersection of Social Categories." *Nature Neuroscience* 19, no. 6 (May 2016): 795–97.

Chapter 2

Bascandziev, Igor, and Paul L. Harris. "The Beautiful and the Accurate: Are Children's Selective Trust Decisions Biased?" *Journal of Experimental Child Psychology* 152 (December 2016): 92–105.

Banaji, Mahzarin R., and Anthony G. Greenwald. *Blindspot: Hidden Biases of Good People*. New York: Delacorte Press, 2013.

Bonilla-Silva, Eduardo. *Racism without Racists: Color-Blind Racism and the Persistence of Racial Inequality in America*. 4th ed. Lanham, MD: Rowman and Littlefield Publishers, 2014.

Correll, Joshua, Sean Hudson, Steffanie Guillermo, and Debbie Ma. "The Police Officer's Dilemma: A Decade of Research on Racial Bias in the Decision to Shoot." *Social and Personality Psychology Compass* 8, no. 5 (May 2014): 201–13.

Dardenne, Benoit, Muriel Dumont, and Thierry Bollier. "Insidious Dangers of Benevolent Sexism: Consequences for Women's Performance." *Journal of Personality and Social Psychology* 93, no. 5 (November 2007): 764–79.

Gaertner, Samuel, and Leonard Bickman. "Effects of Race on the Elicitation of Helping Behavior: The Wrong Number Technique." *Journal of Personality and Social Psychology* 20, no. 2 (November 1971): 218–22.

Geary, Aidan. "Ignored to Death: Brian Sinclair's Death Caused by Racism, Inquest Inadequate, Group Says." CBC News, September 19, 2017. Accessed April 11, 2018. http://www.cbc.ca/news/canada/manitoba/winnipeg-brian-sinclair-report-1.4295996.

Nel, Philip. *Was the Cat in the Hat Black?: The Hidden Racism of Children's Literature, and the Need for Diverse Books.* New York: Oxford University Press, 2017.

Swami, Viren, E. Arthey, and A. Furnham. "Perceptions of Plagiarisers: The Influence of Target Physical Attractiveness, Transgression Severity, and Sex on Attributes of Guilt and Punishment." *Body Image* 22 (September 2017): 144–47.

Washington Post. "Fatal Force, 2017." Database from the website of the *Washington Post*. Accessed April 10, 2018. https://www.washingtonpost.com/graphics/national/police-shootings-2017.

Chapter 3

Cheryan, Sapna, Andrew N. Meltzoff, and Saenam Kim. "Classrooms Matter: The Design of Virtual Classrooms Influences Gender Disparities in Computer Science Classes." *Computers & Education* 57, no. 2 (2011): 1825–35.

Cheryan, Sapna. "Stereotypes as Gatekeepers." TEDx Talks, April 27, 2010. Accessed April 26, 2018. https://youtu.be/TYwl-qM20x4.

Gates, Henry Louis, and Claude M. Steele. "A Conversation with Claude M. Steele." *Du Bois Review: Social Science Research on Race* 6, no. 2 (September 2009): 251–71.

Khosravi, Shahram. "White Masks/Muslim Names: Immigrants and Name-Changing in Sweden." *Race and Class* 53, no. 3 (January 2012): 65–80.

Lyons, Emily McLaughlin, Nina Simma, Kreshnik N. Begolli, and Lindsey E. Richland. "Stereotype Threat Effects on Learning From a Cognitively Demanding Mathematics Lesson." *Cognitive Science* 42, no. 2 (March 2018): 678–90.

Steele, Claude M. *Whistling Vivaldi: And Other Clues to How Stereotypes Affect Us*. New York: W. W. Norton & Company, 2010.

Chapter 4

Black Lives Matter (website). Accessed May 14, 2018. https://blacklivesmatter.com.

Brown, Lyn Mikel, Sharon Lamb, and Mark Tappan. *Packaging Boyhood: Saving Our Sons from Superheroes, Slackers, and Other Media Stereotypes.* New York: St. Martin's Press, 2009.

Coyne, Sarah M., Jennifer Ruh Linder, Eric E. Rasmussen, David A. Nelson, and Victoria Birkbeck. "Pretty as a Princess: Longitudinal Effects of Engagement with Disney Princesses on Gender Stereotypes, Body Esteem, and Prosocial Behaviour in Children." *Child Development* 87, no. 6 (June 2016): 1909–25.

Elmasry, Mohamad Hamas, and Mohammed el-Nawawy. "Do Black Lives Matter?: A Content Analysis of *New York Times* and *St. Louis Post-Dispatch* Coverage of Michael Brown Protests." *Journalism Practice* 11, no. 7 (August 2016): 857–75.

Erisen, Cengiz, Milton Lodge, and Charles S. Taber. "Affective Contagion in Effortful Political Thinking." *Political Psychology* 35, no. 2 (April 2014): 187–206.

Leopold, Joy, and Myrtle P. Bell. "News Media and the Racialization of Protest: An Analysis of Black Lives Matter Articles." *Equality, Diversity and Inclusion* 36, no. 8 (November 2017): 720–35.

Perreaux, Les. "Quebec Mosque Shooter Told Police He Was Motivated by Canada's Immigration Policies." *Globe and Mail,* April 13, 2018.

Reich, Stephanie, Rebecca W. Black, and Tammie Foliaki. "Constructing Difference: Lego® Set Narratives Promote Stereotypic Gender Roles and Play." *Sex Roles* 79, nos. 5–6 (September 2018): 285–98.

Weisgram, Erica S., Megan Fulcher, and Lisa M. Dinella. "Pink Gives Girls Permission: Exploring the Roles of Explicit Gender Labels and Gender-Typed Colors on Preschool Children's Toy Preferences." *Journal of Applied Developmental Psychology* 35, no. 5 (September 2014): 401–9.

Chapter 5

Blair, Irene V., John F. Steiner, and Edward Havranek. "Unconscious (Implicit) Bias and Health Disparities: Where Do We Go from Here?" *The Permanente Journal* 15, no. 2 (Spring 2011): 71–78.

Bonilla-Silva, Eduardo. *Racism without Racists: Color-Blind Racism and the Persistence of Racial Inequality in America*. 4th ed. Lanham, MD: Rowman and Littlefield Publishers, 2014.

Devine, Patricia G., Patrick S. Forscher, Anthony J. Austin, and William T. L. Cox. "Long-term Reduction in Implicit Race Bias: A Predjudice Habit-Breaking Intervention." *Journal of Experimental Social Psychology* 48, no. 6 (November 2012): 1267–78.

Fortunate Eagle, Adam. "The Legal Adventures of Fortunate Eagle: The Activist Formerly Known as Adam Nordwall." *St. Thomas Law Review* 10 (Fall 1997): 53–72.

Freeman, Richard B., and Wei Huang. "Collaboration: Strength in Diversity." *Nature* 513, no. 7518 (September 2014): 305.

Goldin, Claudia, and Cecilia Rouse. "Orchestrating Impartiality: The Impact of 'Blind' Auditions on Female Musicians." *The American Economic Review* 90, no. 4 (September 2000): 715–41.

Maddux, William W., and Adam Galinsky. "Cultural Borders and Mental Barriers: The Relationship Between Living Abroad and Creativity." *Journal of Personality and Social Psychology* 96, no. 5 (May 2009): 1047–61.

Munger, Kevin. "Tweetment Effects on the Tweeted: Experimentally Reducing Racist Harrassment." *Political Behavior* 39, no. 3 (September 2017): 629–49.

Streiff, Michael B., et al. "The Johns Hopkins Venous Thromboembolism Collaborative: Multidisciplinary Team Approach to Achieve Perfect Prophylaxis." *Journal of Hospital Medicine* 11, no. 2 (December 2016): S8–S14.

Vedantam, Shankar. "The Edge Effect." *Hidden Brain*, NPR, podcast, July 2, 2018. https://www.npr.org/2018/07/02/625426015/the-edge-effect.

Vedantam, Shankar. *The Hidden Brain: How Our Unconscious Minds Elect Presidents, Control Markets, Wage Wars, and Save Our Lives*. New York: Spiegel & Grau, 2010.

Index

Adorno, Theodor, 14–15
advertising, 36, 49, 54, 75, 79
affective contagion, 58–59
Allport, Gordon, 15, 68
ambient belonging, 47
attractiveness halo, 33
Australia, 5, 25, 28, 30, 77
authoritarianism, 15, 58

Banaji, Mahzarin, 24–25
Bar-Haim, Yair, 19
Belgium, 5, 30, 31
Bickman, Leonard, 21–22
Bissonette, Alexandre, 58–59
Black Lives Matter, 55–56, 57
blind auditions, 62–63
Boston Symphony Orchestra, 63
Britain, 10, 28, 30, 33, 39, 63, 64

Canada, 5, 10, 28, 30, 34–35, 46, 58–59,
     69, 71–72
Cheryan, Sapna, 46–47
China, 45
Chineke! Orchestra, 64
Civil Rights Movement, 10, 40
   See also King, Martin Luther, Jr.
clothing, 38, 39, 45, 49
computer science, 46–47, 66
contact hypothesis, 68
Corbett, Mike, 60
Correll, Joshua, 26, 27–29
Covington, George, 60

Darwin, Charles, 8
Davenport, Charles and Gertrude, 11
Davis, Art, 62–63
Devine, Patricia, 70
disabilities, 12, 36, 60
dissociation, 20
Dunham, Yarrow, 17

Edwards, Jordan, 26
environmentalists, 7, 59
Ethiopia, 19
eugenics, 8, 11, 14

Fortunate Eagle, Adam, 72
Freeman, Richard B., 74

Gaertner, Samuel, 21–22
Galinsky, Adam, 73
Galton, Francis, 8
Gandhi, Mahatma, 10, 39
Geisel, Theodor Seuss, 35
gender bias, 9, 17, 18, 30–32, 41, 43, 65, 67
   in business, 30
   in computer science, 46–47
   in politics, 30, 71–72, 76
   in science, 30, 46–47, 70
   in sports, 30
   in toys, 50–52
   See also sexism; women's rights
Germany, 5, 11, 12, 14, 28, 46
Goffman, Erving, 23
Greenwald, Anthony, 24–25
gun violence, 5, 26–29, 55, 58–59
   See also under racial bias

health care, 5, 34–35, 55, 65–66
Hitler, Adolf, 11–12
Huang, Wei, 74

Iceland, 28
immigration, 10, 11, 19, 44, 55, 58
Implicit Association Test (IAT), 24–26, 67, 70
implicit bias, 13, 19, 24–27, 33, 35, 61
    in health care, 34–35, 65–66, 68, 77
    in law, 67
    in news media, 57
    in police work, 26–29, 68, 77
impression management, 22–23
India, 10, 39
Indigenous people, 5, 28, 34–35, 54, 65, 72
intergroup bias, 17
International Paralympic Committee, 60
Israel, 19, 69
Italy, 72, 76

Japan, 10, 25, 28, 46
Jehovah's Witnesses, 12
Jewish people, 12, 13, 14–15, 69
Johns Hopkins Hospital, 66

King, Martin Luther, Jr., 76

Latinx people, 54, 63
Lego, 51–52
LGBTQ+ people, 5, 12, 34, 45, 55
Lippmann, Walter, 9–10
Lo, Malinda, 36

Maddux, William, 73
Martin, Trayvon, 55
McClung, Nellie, 71–72
media, 30, 36, 54, 56–57
meditation, 67
Munger, Kevin, 74–75
Muslim people, 25, 44, 45, 58

Nazi party, 12, 14
New Dawn, 53–54
New York Human Rights Commission, 62–63
New York Philharmonic, 62–63
New Zealand, 28
Norway, 28
Nosek, Brian, 24
Nwanoku, Chi-chi, 64

Oh, Ellen, 36
Oliver, Roy, 26
out-group homogeneity effect, 16

Palestinian people, 69
Paluck, Betsy Levy, 54
plastic surgery, 45
Ploetz, Alfred, 11
police, 25, 51, 58, 68, 70, 77, 78
    and protests, 55, 57
    violence, 5, 26, 28–29, 30
Pope, McKenna, 52
Pride celebrations, 55
princess culture, 50
protests, 10, 39, 40, 49, 55–57, 59, 60
    portrayal by media, 56–57

racial bias, 13, 21–22, 24, 25, 34–36, 40–43,
    65, 67
    in babies, 19
    and gun violence, 26–29, 55
    in orchestras, 62–64
    See also Black Lives Matter; gun violence
racism, 14–15, 21–23, 24, 26, 35–36,
    40, 78
    in health care, 5, 34–35, 65
    on social media, 74–75
refugees, 58, 79
Roma people, 12, 54
Rwanda, 53–54, 77

Schallmayer, Wilhelm, 11
Seeds of Peace camp, 69
senior citizens, 7, 37, 43
Seuss, Dr. *See* Geisel, Theodor Seuss
sexism, 24, 30–32, 61
    benevolent, 31–32
    See also gender bias; women's rights
Sinclair, Brian, 34, 65
slavery, 9, 64
social media, 32, 36, 74–75, 78
Somalia, 54
South Korea, 46
Steele, Claude, 40–43, 47
stereotype lift, 44
stereotype replacement, 70
stereotype threat, 40–43, 44, 47–48, 65
Stonewall Riots, 55
Sweden, 5, 25, 44–45, 77

Tel Aviv University, 19
Trudeau, Justin, 58
Trump, Donald, 55, 58

United States, 9, 13, 54, 55, 60, 62–63, 65,
    66, 69
    police violence, 5, 26, 28–29
    research, 15, 22, 27–29, 30, 63, 70
    women's rights, 10

Vacher de Lapouge, Georges, 11

Wellman, Mark, 60
We Need Diverse Books, 36
Williams Syndrome, 18
women's rights, 10, 55, 71–72
    Women's March, 55, 56
    See also gender bias
World War II, 12, 14, 58